AMERICA'S BEST TRAILS

AMERICA'S BEST TRAILS

THE MOST BEAUTIFUL PLACES TO RUN

BY JEFF GALLOWAY & BRENNAN GALLOWAY

Meyer & Meyer Sport

British Library Cataloguing in Publication Data
A catalogue record for this book is available from the British Library

America's Best Trails
Maidenhead: Meyer & Meyer Sport (UK) Ltd., 2016
ISBN 978-1-78255-096-9

© 2016 by Meyer & Meyer Sport (UK) Ltd.
2nd revised edition
Aachen, Auckland, Beirut, Cairo, Cape Town, Dubai, Hägendorf, Hong Kong,
Indianapolis, Manila, New Delhi, Singapore, Sydney, Tehran, Vienna

 Member of the World Sport Publishers' Association (WSPA)
www.w-s-p-a.org

Manufacturing: Print Consult GmbH, Munich, Germany
ISBN 978-1-78255-096-9
E-Mail: info@m-m-sports.com
www.m-m-sports.com

Table of Contents

Preface

by Barbara Galloway

Anthropologists tell us that humans evolved as endurance animals. We survived because we as a species developed the internal programming and physical conditioning to keep moving for hours, days, and weeks at a time. Because our ancestors walked, ran, and sprinted on natural terrain, we enhance the fitness and empowerment of running by going back to our roots. The most exciting research today shows that while we experience a treasury of health and physical benefits from running, the mental and psychological rewards are even more significant: quicker decisions, better judgment, improved attitude, more vitality.

Running on trails revs up brain activity another notch, while also allowing us to "be in the moment." Running on trails forces us to touch the earth on every step and to be constantly aware. We must process a variety of information, adjust to the surface, elevation, weather, vegetation, and be ready for what comes ahead. The good news is that we inherited from our ancestors all of the capabilities to do this, while receiving the rewards.

My most memorable runs have been on trails. I've come to embrace the never-ending stream of invigorating challenges, stresses, and minor risks which bring the significant and continuing rewards of being alert, mentally fresh, and energized to take action. Running changes your brain. Trail running enhances these changes. As a result, I have found myself better able to appreciate, respond, and adapt to the challenges and opportunities in other areas of life.

Introduction

Meet Brennan Galloway

It's a joy for me to co-author this book with my son, Brennan. Even during the first few months of his life, Brennan was covering dozens of miles every month on the Kennesaw Mountain National Park trail system. His mom, Barbara, and I wore out the first version of the "baby jogger" on these forest trails with Brennan wide awake, absorbing the natural forest environment, downloading the sounds, smells, and terrain. When he started running and hiking with our Tahoe Running Retreat folks, Brennan was a natural on trails at age 4.

While competing in cross country and track at Colorado College, Brennan ran countless miles on trails. He also produced a documentary on one of the top ultra marathoners in the world, Anton Krupica, who is a friend.

Brennan and his wife, Jenny, travelled extensively throughout the US, running on most of the trails and taking photos. While they contributed most of the photos, other photographers have contributed and are mentioned in the appropriate section.

Jeff Galloway

PART I

PART I: Trail-Specific Training

1 A Trail Is Not a Road

1.1 What Qualifies as a Best Run?

When Brennan and I look back at what we consider our best runs, almost all of them were trails. It's not just the scenery. As you move along a trail, through forest, desert, parkland, you enter a different state of mind. You're constantly interacting with the ground, vegetation, elevation change, and a variety of sounds and aromas. Mind–body activity is elevated to a higher level of awareness to be ready to react. You're living in the moment and interacting with real life around you as you move forward.

There is something primitive and restorative when running on the trail. Our ancestors programmed us to keep going for days at a time because survival depended upon doing so. As we move down along a natural trail, we go back to our roots in a positive way. Barbara cited the mental and psychological benefits in the preface. The bottom line is that we almost always feel better after a trail run with a sense of connecting to our environment and other living creatures.

Sharing. There's a special bond that occurs when we run with one or more companions along a trail. We're turning on circuits that connect us with millions of years of evolution. The extra trust and cooperation you feel toward a trail running companion often extends after the run. Some runners communicate and bond better on trails—even when nothing is said—than when running other venues. Trail companions are connected in ancient and satisfying ways, pulling one another along to get through tough situations.

Variety. Even if you run the same trail each day you will feel different sensations on each run—because of changes in lighting, seasons, and weather. When you choose a different trail every month, you will enhance your running experience and look forward to each adventure. One of the missions of this book is to introduce you to 50 interesting running venues. Don't keep these to yourself—spread the word.

The mission. Planning for trail runs connects you to the history and geography of the area. It's fun to find interesting places to stay, eat, and explore. As you coordinate with travel companions you'll create a special life experience—not just a running experience.

Enjoyable scenery. Most of the trails we selected for this book have scenic sections. Some are spectacular, others offer a series of natural scenes that are enjoyable in themselves with visual images, interesting and diverse sounds, mysteries, and puzzles. Surprising are the discoveries during runs on trails that at first seem boring or unstimulating. Within a few minutes you'll see details of ground cover, vegetation, animal prints or signs, and sounds made by the wind or vegetation. You could write several pages about the details seen and felt along every segment of just about any trail.

Strengthening of legs and feet. The feet and legs have to work a bit harder on trails to maintain balance, push off on different terrain, and shift usage of muscles. All of the adaptations for adjusting to various surfaces are embedded in us. As we run regularly on non-paved surfaces we get better and better at adjusting pace, foot placement, inserting walk breaks, and moving around hazards. You find a different sense of balance on trails. Muscles and tendons intuitively strengthen and work together in special ways during different segments of each trail. You'll often notice when a road runner spends a year training on trails, many of the small leg muscles acquire greater definition.

Part of nature. As you move through the trees, plants, hills, grass, or sand, you become part of nature—picking up bits of the forest, field, valley, or prairie. You're literally grounded as you touch earth on each step. You feel and wear the moisture (or lack of) and collect the dust, mist, snow, frost, or dew.

Preparation for off-road races. A growing number of races offer off-road races or segments. As you train on trails that simulate your race course, you adapt the feet, legs, and balance for the exact demands of the race itself. Many who run trail events will schedule trips to train on the course in advance and reduce the surprises on race day. The best preparation for running on a trail is to train on that trail.

View scenery in a unique way. Due to the lighting, foliage, or recent precipitation, each scene on a trail run is different from any other. Many runners carry cameras or phones and capture images that are revisited over and over, often turning the photos into screensavers. But most of the images are stored away in the memory cells. Every week, during a run, a certain image, shadow, or cloud formation will bring flashes of my rich memories in the Sierra mountains, Arizona desert preserves, or a Florida pine forest. Some were experienced last week but others decades ago—a wonderful and direct connection with our running past.

Brain invigoration. The brain instinctively revs up when you start running on a trail, turning on circuits for high awareness. From ancient times, running directly on the earth required more resources from the mind–body network. The central nervous system is on high alert, reflexes are ready to respond, energy circuits gear up to conserve and then deliver as needed. Muscles are activated, performance hormones are released, and mechanical units flow into a smooth range of motion. I know of no other activity that activates our vitality and positive expectations than trail running.

The result is that I feel more alive and energized when running down a trail: body, mind, and spirit working together. Brennan and I wish you many special trail experiences.

1.2 Glossary of Trail Terms

Note: Thanks to Kerry Dycus, Chris Twiggs, and Dave James for their input on these terms.

Trailhead – A location where you can access a trail. Sometimes there is parking and other services. If located in a national or state park, there may be a user fee. Paying the fee supports upkeep and trail development.

Out and back – Running along a trail in one direction for a certain distance, then running back to the start.

Loop trail – A trail that starts and finishes at the same place but has little or no duplication of the route—making a circle.

Point to point – A route that starts in one place and finishes in a different place. Transportation logistics are necessary when setting up such routes.

Single track – This trail is only wide enough for one person at a time. Runners have to yield to other runners to let them pass. Make sure that you leave enough space between you and the runner ahead.

Double track – A two-lane trail that is made by an ATV or truck, for example. Running side by side is possible, passing is easy, and two-way traffic is not a problem. Keep right; pass on the left.

Technical – Trails that have lots of rocks, roots, elevation issues, and ditches. Technical trails require a lot more attention than most because foot placement is extremely important. They may also include switchbacks, sharp turns, or blind corners. Technical trails require a delicate balance of looking ahead and looking at the ground ahead of you to avoid tripping. As always, take an extra walk break to reduce risks and see what's ahead.

Switchback – A section of trail that makes a zigzag up or down a hill. This is particularly found when there is a very steep elevation change and is usually preferable to running straight up or down.

Trail etiquette – This has become an extremely important topic lately as more and more people are taking up trail running. Runners, hikers, cyclists, and sometimes horses will be sharing the same trail. Be aware of the other creatures ahead of and behind you.

* Passing. When approaching someone who is slower, let them know you are there with a cough or a greeting, such as "How's it going?" Politely thank the yielding runner as you go by after he or she pulls to the side. Uphill runners should yield to downhill runners. The downhill runner has gravity and momentum on his or her side—don't get in the way of either of these. "Passing left" is the best way to let another runner know that you plan to come by, but the person in front needs to be aware that there are faster runners behind them as well. For this reason, a lot of trail races forbid headphones.
* Be patient! When approaching slower runners on a narrow path, don't put yourself or the other runners at risk. It is appropriate to ask, "could I please get ahead of you?"
* Being passed. When running on single track, be aware of those behind who are running faster than you and want to pass. Many single-track races don't have many passing opportunities. When faster runners come up from behind, step aside so that they can pass.
* Be "green." Please carry your trash with you (gel packs, wrappers, water bottles). Fatigue can result in sloppiness which can lead to litter on the trail.
* When running with your dog: Use a leash. Even a friendly dog can cause other runners to fall. Always scoop the poop.
* Stay on the trail! Obey posted signs and don't cut switchbacks. Some countries do not have the same rules for nature preservation as we do in the United States. If you are competing in a race outside the US, switchback cutting may be allowed, but it's best for the environment to stay on the established trail.

* Buddy system: The safest trail running, just like the safest road running, is with a buddy. But if you run alone, make sure someone knows your planned route and when to expect you back. Bring your cell phone.

1.3 Caution! Rough Road Ahead—The Unique Challenges

Rules of the Trail
1. Run with a buddy or two.
2. Bring a cell phone.
3. Research the area for risks—and avoid them.
4. Wear adequate clothing.
5. Walk gently through hazards.

Who should not run trails? Those of us who love running on trails want all of our friends to enjoy it. Unfortunately, some will be miserable or will suffer repeat injuries when running in the natural environment. By gradually introducing the feet, legs, and psyche to trail running there is a chance that even those who hated trails at first will become trail lovers. But everyone needs to be careful in the beginning.

Weak ankles put one at risk on uneven terrain. Those with very mobile ankle joints are very likely to suffer ankle sprains, strains, and tendon irritation in other areas. I've run with some weak-ankle runners, and just about any irregularity can set off the movement that can cause aggravation and injury.

Foot, knee, and hip issues can be triggered by uneven terrain. More walking and strengthening exercises can reduce the risk, but those who have repeat injuries in these areas should look to a pedestrian or bike trail system, with a paved surface, when they take to the trails.

Some runners are anxious when they run away from "civilization." The fear of the unknown is real and will leave anxious runners with a negative feeling after a trail run. Gradually venturing into woods or parks can sometimes allow runners to adapt and desensitize the emotions. But running with an experienced and supportive companion(s) can also deal with this.

If you are running with someone who is challenged by any of these issues, talk about the problems and make sure the novice has medical clearance to run on rough terrain.

Buddy system. Always go with another person. Accidents happen to the most experienced trail runners, and no one is exempt from unexpected adverse weather and unexpected terrain. Those who run alone are putting themselves at risk in several threatening areas: encountering wildlife, getting lost, or experiencing a medical emergency.

Shoes. Do some research on the trail you will be running. This will help you choose what shoes to wear. Many trails allow for regular running shoes. Those who have unstable ankles should wear shoes that are lower to the ground when running on trails. When there is gravel or sharp objects, trail shoes with foot protection can help. Ask some veteran trail runners who have used the trail you will be running—or shoe store staff who are very knowledgeable about trail shoes.

Look ahead and walk when the surface is questionable. While running, we often rely on momentum to maintain balance. This can get us into trouble when we try to run through a trail segment with lots of debris. Keep looking ahead on the trail for possible surface hazards. Always err on the safe side by walking gently to maintain control when the surface is questionable.

Getting lost? Some runners don't have a good sense of direction. When running in a group of two or more, make sure that one member knows the trail really well or has an excellent sense of direction. Just to be sure, bring some brightly colored plastic flagging ribbon (sometimes called surveyors tape) and mark the trail at regular intervals. The ribbons will be very helpful when you are returning through an intersection of trails. As you move away from each ribbon, look back and visualize what you will see when you are returning.

Carry a cell phone—with reception. Every year a number of runners and hikers are saved because they brought their cell phones. Make sure that the phone can be used in the area you are running.

Carry a flashlight—just in case. Those who run in early morning or at dusk tend to bring flashlights. It only takes one wrong turn, and you could be in the wilderness when the sun goes down.

1.4 Trail Safety

Each year I hear of serious accidents experienced by dozens of trail runners. Most of them are preventable. Here are the primary causes and what you can do about them.

1. Sometimes runners don't focus on the surface.
   Always be on guard—even when the trail seems to be smooth and comfortable. Be aware of anything that could cause a fall and avoid it. If there are a series of surface challenges, walk slowly or stop and set up a plan for getting through the areas.
   Be aware of your surroundings. I know it is wonderful to be on "cruise control" in your right brain, but you need to be aware of the path ahead to avoid a dangerous fall. Just keep looking around and anticipating.
   When running or walking with another person, don't try to follow blindly on the trail. Allow for 30 feet or so between you and the runner ahead. This allows you to see the surface and take action. Runners who pick up the pace around a curve can be surprised when they round the corner. Be cautious. Look at the side of the trail and have an option for diversion if the surface is slippery or there are unexpected obstacles.

2. Sometimes, runners get distracted by conversation or scenery. One of the very positive aspects of running becomes a negative one, in this case. Yes, chat and enjoy time with your friends. But every runner in a group needs to be responsible for his or her own safety and footing. Runners at the back of a group should never assume that they don't have to be concerned about hazards at all. Be responsible for your own safety.

3. In general, be ready to save yourself from a variety of trail problems by following the rules listed. Even if the rules seem obvious, many runners incur serious injuries on trails when they ignore them.

4. Be aware of the health and fitness ability of your running companions. You don't want someone to get into a challenge that could leave them without energy or muscle power to run out of the forest.

5. Go over the trail map regularly and check the map. Make notes so that you can retrace your steps if you get lost. Think ahead at all times, and create a plan for any challenge.

6. Bring lights on all afternoon runs. Some runners get lost on trails and have to find their way back in the dark.

7. Take control of your safety—you are the best person on the trail who can keep yourself safe.

1.5 Equipment

To prepare for various challenges along the trail, you'll need supplies. Listed in this chapter are the key items used by trail runners. As you get more experienced, you will add individual items.

Make a list and check it twice. Keep a running list of items, with your belt or pack, to make it easy to do an inventory before each run. When you return, replace items used and add to the list when you think of another item that would be helpful.

You don't need all of these items on every run. On short trail runs, where you know your way, you may not need any of them. But when in doubt, bring it!

Trail Checklist
* Supply/hydration belt—I like the small elastic belt products which have hydration holsters and pouches. You want one that stays snug around the waist. I love the bib holder which eliminates pinning bib numbers on shirts in races. For very long runs where water is not available, the camelback products are popular. The large bladder of water is carried like a backpack, and you can use a tube to suck the water you need.
* Backpack—To comfortably carry what you need. There are many different versions at running stores and outdoor stores.
* Cell phone—Make sure it is charged.
* GPS—In case the area is confusing, for exploring a new trail, or if you get lost.
* Flashlight—If you might be running at dusk or in the dark.
* Flagging—To mark the right trail at an intersection on your return.
* Bring water—Especially on runs longer than 90 minutes. (Don't drink water from streams or lakes.)
* H_2O rule of thumb: 2-4 oz. of water every two miles.
* Snacks—Especially on runs longer than 90 minutes.
* Blood sugar boosting rule of thumb: 30-40 calories every two miles.

* Map of area—If there are many intersections of trails, a map of the area is recommended.
* Pepper spray—If you suspect that wild animals could be in the area.
* First aid kit—band aids, Neosporin, antiseptic wipes, individual items.
* Bug spray—If there are mosquitoes or other bugs that bite or sting.
* Sunscreen—Towelettes or wipes.
* Poison ivy/poison oak prevention and treatment.
* Garbage bags—In case of rain. (Cut a hole for the head).
* Gaiters—To keep debris out of your shoes.
* Compression sleeves—For faster recovery and protection from poison ivy/oak and briars.
* Technical equipment for special trails.
* Gripping gloves and shoes.

2 Choosing the Right Trail

Trails vary greatly in difficulty. Some are flat, gentle, without confusing cross trails. Other trail systems are full of rocks, roots, erosion, and other hazards. It pays to do your trail homework.

* Some trails become a lot more difficult during and after a rain storm. Ask whether certain areas are prone to flash floods, quicksand, mudslides, or rock slides. Be aware of possible falling branches.
* Consult local trail runners. A good local running store or running club can probably help you connect with local trail runners. Tell the expert the type of trail you would like to run—and hazards you'd like to avoid.
* Find a map! Some running and outdoor stores have trail maps. You may also find these at the local office of your state or US Forest Service or state or National Park office. The websites of many state and National parks and forests will often have trail maps.
* Be aware of animal threats. Ask if there have been sightings of aggressive animals such as bears, mountain lions, wild hogs,

wild dogs, etc. In wilderness areas, moose and even deer have been known to run over humans, resulting in significant injury and death.

* Are there poisonous snakes, spiders, or other threats? If so, find out where they have been seen, how to avoid contact, and what time of the day is best to avoid them.

* Some insects carry diseases such as lime disease or West Nile virus. The local health department usually tracks cases of such afflictions and where they were acquired.

* Are you allergic to any plants or shrubs in the area? If so, cover yourself and reduce the possible skin contact. Carry medication in case you need it—to reduce the downtime. If you have problems with poison ivy or poison oak, look up pictures of leaf design and structure, and be vigilant. Cover exposed skin.

* Make sure the trail area is safe. Most local trail runners can tell you about safety issues that are not covered here. Ask if cars have been broken into at the trailhead—or if other crime has been observed in the area.

Trail Challenges

After talking to trail runners, mark possible challenges on your trail map. Before beginning your trail run, note the hazardous places. If there are a continuing series of hazards, break out the map every 10-15 minutes and look at the next trail segment.

Prevention is the best strategy to avoid ankle sprains or other injuries. Walk carefully through uneven areas, and you can reduce your risk.

Rocks—Shoes only help to a certain point. When the surface is too unstable, you should walk carefully.

Roots—It is easy to trip when there are a lot of roots in the area. It's best to walk and stay focused on each root ahead.

Ruts—Water erosion can change a smooth trail into a very rugged one in an hour or two.

Hidden risks—During fall and winter, leaves can cover potholes, rocks, and other trail obstacles. Walk through potentially hazardous areas.

Steep downhill—It is common to slip on dirt, sand, rocks, or slick rock face when running downhill. Manage your pace by walking before you get out of control.

Flash floods—Note the low places on your map and work out a strategy to escape if it starts raining. If your map has contour lines you can find higher ground. Beware of a flooded area—you don't know how deep the water is.

Slippery surface—Where there is water, your footing can be unexpectedly slippery. Situations that should trigger careful footing include the following: near creeks, rock faces that have drainage, or during or after a rain (even a light rain).

Lightning—During a lightning storm, it's best to take cover—and avoid higher elevations.

Where do runners tend to get lost? Most experienced trail runners can tell you. Mark your maps and then use flagging tape to mark the correct trail. The correct path looks different on the way back.

3 The Galloway Run-Walk-Run Method

3.1 Better Control on Uneven Terrain

The right run-walk-run strategy on a trail run allows you to be more resilient at the end of tiring runs, with less fatigue. You can carry on your life activities after long runs. By taking strategic walk breaks in the first few miles, you will have more leg strength and resiliency for the last few miles.

Walk before you get tired.
Most of us, even when untrained, can walk for several miles before fatigue sets in, because walking is an activity that we can do efficiently for hours. Running is more work, because you have to lift your body off the ground and then absorb the shock of the landing, over and over. The continuous use of the running muscles will produce much more fatigue, aches, and pains than maintaining the same pace while taking walk breaks. If you walk before your running muscles start to get tired, you allow the muscle to recover instantly—increasing your capacity for exercise while reducing the chance of next-day soreness.

The "method" part involves having a strategy. By using a ratio of running and walking that is right for you on each day, you can manage your fatigue. You are the one who is strong to the finish, doing what you need or want to do after long runs. You never have to be exhausted after a long run again.

This is even more important when running on trails because you have to work harder. Walk breaks will reduce fatigue buildup.

The run-walk-run method is very simple: You run for a short segment and then take a walk break, and keep repeating this pattern.

Walk breaks...
* allow you to have more control when running on rocky, rooty, or slippery trails.
* provide more chances to look around and appreciate the scenery.
* give you control over the way you feel at the end.
* erase fatigue—walk break by walk break.
* push back your fatigue wall.
* allow for endorphins to collect during each walk break—you feel good!
* break up the distance into manageable units ("two more minutes" or "thirty more seconds").
* speed recovery.
* reduce the chance of aches, pains, and injury.
* allow you to feel good afterward—carrying on the rest of your day without debilitating fatigue.
* give you all of the endurance of the distance of each session—without the pain.
* allow older runners or heavier runners to recover fast and feel as good or better as the younger (slimmer) days.
* activate the frontal lobe—keeping you in control over your attitude and motivation.

Use a short and gentle walking stride.
It's better to walk slowly, with a short stride. There has been some irritation

of the shins when runners or walkers maintain a stride that is too long. Relax and enjoy the walk.

3.2 No Need to Eliminate the Walk Breaks

Some beginners assume that they must work toward the day when they don't have to take any walk breaks at all. This is up to the individual, but it is not recommended—especially when running trails. Remember that you decide what ratio of run-walk-run to use. There is no rule that requires you to hold to any ratio on a given day. As you adjust the run-walk-run to how you feel, you gain control over your fatigue.

Adjust walk break amounts and frequency on trails.
Because of terrain and moisture issues, trail runners must be ready to take more frequent walk breaks to gain control over balance. By slowing down and walking at the first sign of debris ahead, you can assess the situation, adjust stride, and maintain control.

The best way to deal with weak ankles, feet, and knees is to prevent problems by walking before you step on something that turns your feet. On rough trails you will be taking more walk breaks.

Falls are a common cause of injury. Runners who try to run through a debris field are more likely to fall on the rocks or roots that caused the fall.

Walk up hills.
It is a common practice among trail runners, in races or training runs, to walk most or all of the hills. Those who have compared their times—walking up a trail hill and then running up the same hill—have found that the time was not significantly different. But the fatigue was a lot greater when running uphill.

I've run for over 50 years, and one of the extra running freedoms on trails is taking walk breaks when you want or need to do so. I enjoy running on trails more than ever because of walk breaks.

Keep track of the walk breaks.

On smooth trails, you can use a timer that tells you when to run and then when to walk. The best product is the Galloway run-walk-run timer, which will beep or vibrate. There are several watches which can be set for two intervals. Check our website: *www.jeffgalloway.com.*

3.3 Run-Walk-Run Ratios on Smooth Trails

After having heard back from more than 300,000 runners who have used walk breaks at various paces, I've come up with the following suggested ratios.

Pace per mile	Run Amount	Walk Amount
7:00	6 minutes	30 seconds (or run a mile/ walk 40 seconds)
7:30	5 minutes	30 seconds
8:00	4 minutes	30 seconds
8:30	4 minutes	45 seconds
9:00	4 minutes	1 minute
9:30	3 minutes	45 seconds
10:00-10:45	3 minutes	1 minute
10:45-11:45	2:30 minutes	1 minute
11:45-12:45	2 minutes	1 minute
12:45-13:30	1 minute	1 minute
13:30-14:30	30 seconds	30 seconds
14:30-15:30	20 seconds	40 seconds
15:30-17:00	15 seconds	45 seconds
17:00-18:30	10 seconds	50 seconds
18:30-20:00	5 seconds	55 seconds

Note: You may always divide each of the amounts by 2. Example: Instead of running 12 minute/mile pace using 2-1, you could run for 1 minute and walk for 30 seconds.

3.4 Adjusting Walk Breaks on Trails

Walk breaks are even more important on long trail runs than on long pavement runs. Not only will the walks allow you to cope with trail hazards, but walking will also help your legs, which, at the end of a trail run, are going to be tired and less able to respond to uneven challenges. I hear from quite a few runners every year who tell me that they could have avoided falls, ankle injuries, and tree impact traumas if they had taken walk breaks more frequently.

Using a run–walk–run timer on smooth sections can help you settle into a rhythm. Our Blue Mountain Beach (FL) retreat has mile after mile of mostly stable surface trails, and we use timers. Many runners who don't take the walks according to a rhythm in the beginning tend to get much more tired by the end of the run. Even if you don't feel like you need to take a walk break during the first mile or two, your legs will thank you later if you do so.

But on most trails, the walk breaks will be taken as needed, as noted. Because you are facing unknown footing on most trails, it's best to walk at the first sign of a hazard. On rugged trails, watch for rough terrain, slippery surfaces, unknown surfaces, or frequent holes. By walking before you get into risky footing you not only reduce your rate of injury, but you also allow the muscles to recover before severe fatigue sneaks up on you. In the process, you gain control over your run.

Running form can help you stay under control and stable. Shorten stride down to baby steps if needed. Keep your feet underneath you at all times. As long as you clear the obstacles on the ground, don't bounce off the ground, but rather use a light touch of the foot. Using these form suggestions can allow you to slow down, stop, or make side-to-side movements more easily—when needed.

Walk through uneven surfaces. Be prepared at any time to slow down and walk. Keep looking ahead, sizing up the potential surface issues. Always err on the side of walking or even stopping to ensure you have stable ground. When leaves and other debris cover the trail, walk carefully until you feel the path is secure.

Slippery when wet! Moisture can make dirt, rocks, and rock faces very slick. Walk carefully through areas that could be risky. When a stream covers the trail, walk around to find a narrow place to cross. If you have to run through the stream, it's usually better to walk through it because you don't know the true surface underneath the water.

Walk up steep hills. It is not only more difficult to run up a hill, but you can't see the surface ahead as well as when running on the flat. It only takes one patch of loose gravel to send you crashing down the hill. When in doubt, be extra careful.

Beware when tired—take extra time to stay under control. At the end of a long run, you will not be able to control feet and legs as you can when fresh. When rocks, slippery surface or holes are present, you're more likely to get injured if you try to run through the hazards.

Primary concept of walk breaks is the same on trails as on pavement: If you take them more frequently and early, you will have better muscle control, more energy, and quicker reflex action later. Even if you have run a trail a hundred times, weather and nature can present you with challenges you did not anticipate. You want to have as many resources as possible when challenged.

4 Terrain Training

Most runners can adapt to running on uneven terrain if they warm up gently, gradually introduce the feet to terrain, and take an extended walk break when there are problems. Many of my e-coaching clients have found that gentle to moderate terrain training has strengthened the lower legs and has reduced ankle problems among those who had such problems.

If you have unstable ankles or a history of foot issues from uneven terrain, you must be ultra-conservative in warming up and when running terrain segments. Follow the instructions below but go into a conservative walk before running over terrain that could cause injuries.

Once your feet, legs, and muscles have adapted to uneven terrain, regular runs on grass, fields, and trails will maintain these adaptations. At least one day a week, during one of your short runs, find a stable area of grass or dirt and run gently for two to four segments of about 5 minutes each.

Warm up by walking for 3-5 minutes on stable terrain. Then, remaining on stable terrain, do a gentle warm-up with more walking than you plan to use later for 3 minutes. During the next 3 minutes, still on stable terrain, gradually ease into the run-walk-run strategy that you will be using later in the run. If all is well, begin your terrain segment with 20-30 seconds on stable grass or dirt, followed by 30-60 seconds of gentle walking to allow the feet and ankles to adapt. Continue to alternate segments three to four times, gradually increasing the roughness of the terrain until it simulates the type of terrain you want to prepare for. Don't get into an uncomfortable situation. Walk for 2-3 minutes gently and start over again, gradually increasing the roughness of the terrain.

Note: Stop the workout and walk if you feel any orthopedic issue.

At first you should do only 5 minutes of these segments. Gradually increase the number of segments until you are doing 5-7 x 5-minute segments. This allows the feet, ankles, and legs to adapt to uneven terrain.

Don't keep running on terrain that could produce injury. Structure the terrain segment so that you have a stable area within a few steps, and move to that area when needed. Don't hesitate to walk as much as needed between terrain segments.

There is no need to run over very rocky and risky terrain. Even in races, you should walk gently through such areas.

If you have not run on uneven terrain for several weeks, ease back into this by using the starter workout first. Those who have problems with unstable terrain need to be careful and should use an even more conservative approach to the terrain than suggested previously. All runners should run these terrain segments slowly during the first few workouts.

5 Hill Training

Top Mistakes Made When Running Hills on Trails

1. Striding too long down a hill
2. Striding too long up a hill
3. Increasing the pace when running up a hill
4. Leaning too far forward when running up a hill
5. Leaning back too far when running down a hill
6. Leaning too far forward when running down a hill
7. Pumping the arms to get up a hill faster
8. Trying to "win the hill"
9. Not taking strategic walk breaks when running up or down a hill
10. Letting gravity pull you down a hill too fast when there is debris on the trail

41

Hill Running Concepts

1. Keep the effort level and breathing rate consistent and conversational as you approach a hill.
2. Touch lightly as you go up the hill. (Many trail runners walk up most or all hills.)
3. If you insert running segments when going uphill, reduce stride length as you run up to maintain resiliency in the leg muscles.
4. Reduce stride to "baby steps" when needed on steep hills or long hills—OR WALK.
5. Monitor effort by breathing rate—try to maintain the same breathing pattern as on the flat.
6. Stay smooth when running up and running down a hill.
7. Let gravity pull you down the hill—as you touch lightly with a relatively short stride.
8. Let cadence or turnover increase as you run down—without a great increase in stride length.
9. Watch for trail hazards constantly and walk through them.
10. Don't overstride!

Uphill Running Form

* Start with a comfortable stride—a shorter stride than you would use on flat terrain.
* As you go up the hill, shorten the stride further.
* Touch lightly with your feet.
* Maintain a body posture that is perpendicular to the horizontal (upright, not leaning forward or back).
* Pick up the turnover of your feet as you go up and over the top.
* Keep adjusting your stride so that the leg muscles don't tighten up—you want them as resilient as possible as you adapt to the debris.
* Relax as you go over the top of the hill, and glide (or coast) on the downside, minimizing effort.

Downhill Form

* Maintain a light touch of the foot.
* Use an average stride—or quick shuffle.
* Keep feet low to the ground.
* Let gravity pull you down the hill.
* Turnover of the feet will pick up.
* Try to glide (or coast) quickly down the hill.
* Take strategic walk breaks if you feel the need.
* Constantly watch for trail surface irregularities and adjust.

Hill Training for Strength and Race Preparation

Even if your next trail race is on relatively flat terrain, you will encounter a hill at some point.

Hill training is the best leg strengthening exercise for any type of running. By doing a regular series of hill workouts you can develop the foot and leg adaptations needed for running various types of hills.

With the added strength from hill training, you can adjust to an efficient stride, run more efficiently, and reduce wear and tear on the muscles at the end of all runs. You'll also improve your hill running technique in races.

The hill training workouts are not designed to result in exhaustion. They should gently introduce the feet, legs, and cardiovascular system to uphills and downhills, while improving muscle strength and running efficiency.

Terrain?

The main benefits of hill training, listed previously, can be achieved by running hills on paved surface: sidewalks, park asphalt trails, streets, overpasses, bridges. We recommend running hill sessions on stable surface and not on rough terrain.

5.1 The Hill Workout

* Walk for 2-3 minutes.
* Jog and walk to a hill—about 10 minutes. Beginners should jog a minute and walk a minute (a longer warm-up is fine) during the first few weeks of training.
* Reverse this warm-up as you cool down.
* Choose a hill with an easy or moderate grade—steep hills often cause problems.
* Run up the hill for 5 seconds and then down for 5 seconds, gently. Walk for 15-20 seconds. Repeat this 5-10 times. This finalizes the warm-up.
* Walk for 2-3 minutes.
* Run the first few steps of each hill acceleration at a jog, then gradually pick up the turnover of the feet as you go up the hill.
* Get into a comfortable rhythm so that you can gradually increase this turnover (# of steps per minute) as you go up the hill.
* Keep shortening stride length as you go up the hill.
* It's OK to huff and puff at the top of the hill (due to increased turnover and running uphill), but don't let the legs get over extended, or feel exhausted.
* Run over the top of the hill by at least four steps.
* Jog back to the top of the hill and walk down to recover between the hills. Walk as much as you need for complete recovery after each hill.

Hill Workout Running Form
* Start with a comfortable stride—fairly short.
* As you go up the hill, shorten the stride.
* Touch lightly with your feet.
* Maintain a body posture that is perpendicular to the horizon (upright, not leaning forward or back).
* Pick up the turnover of your feet as you go up and over the top. (It's OK to huff and puff as you go up the hill.)
* Keep adjusting stride so that the leg muscles don't tighten up—you want them as resilient as possible.

* Relax as you go over the top of the hill, and glide (or coast) a bit on the downside.

Hill training strengthens lower legs and improves running form.
The incline of the hill forces your legs to work harder as you go up. The extra work up the incline and the faster turnover builds strength. By taking an easy walk between the hills, and an easy day afterward, the lower-leg muscles rebuild stronger. Over several months, the improved strength allows you to support your body weight farther forward on your feet. An extended range of motion of the ankle and Achilles tendon results in a "bonus" extension of the foot forward—with no increase in effort. You will run faster without working harder. What a deal!

5.2 Saving Strength for the End of Trail Runs

By doing regular hill training, you will not be as challenged during trail hills or as fatigued at the end. This will reduce the chance of wobble injuries which occur when a fatigued foot or leg assumes a sloppy range of motion.

Once you train yourself to run with efficient hill form, you'll gain more confidence when you encounter hills during a race and build strength to handle any hill. Hill training allows you to cruise up a hill without the degree of huffing and puffing that you used to experience. In other words, hill workouts will make running uphill almost as natural as running on the flat. When you come to a hill on a trail run you won't have to work as hard and will not be as tired at the end.

5.3 Biggest Mistakes: Too Long a Stride and Bouncing Too Much

Even when the stride is one or two inches too long, your downhill speed can get out of control. If you are bouncing more than an inch or two off the ground, you run the risk of pounding your feet, having to use your quads to slow down (producing soreness), and creating hamstring soreness due to overstriding. Best indicator of overstriding is having tight hamstrings (the big muscles behind your upper leg) and sore quads the next day. Using a quick and slightly shorter stride allows you to control downhill speed and better foot placement. You'll also reduce the chance of sore quads, sore shins, or aggravated hamstrings.

PART II

PART II: Trails and Races

6 Scenic Races

There are different types of beauty, and then there is the "eye of the beholder." Having run in over 1,000 events over my 50-plus years of running, I've come to appreciate the races that have a special combination of scenic qualities. Here they are.

Big Sur International Marathon

Carmel/Monterey, CA

Usually the last weekend in April.

Photos by Reg Regalado

I've not run any course that has more dramatic views of the natural coastal environment as the Big Sur International Marathon. While running this course I've seen whales, sea lions with pups, various hawks, and a variety of other animals, wild and domesticated.

The topographical relief is dramatic. Within a short distance of the ocean is Big Sur's Cone Peak—the highest coastal mountain in the lower 48 states at 5,155 feet elevation. The Big Sur section of this road (US 1) took 18 years to build and opened in the late 1930s.

Starting in the tall trees of Pfeiffer Big Sur State Park in the community of Big Sur Village, the undulating course passes ranches, state parks, the Point Sur lighthouse, Hurricane Point, spectacular Bixby Bridge, Palo Colorado Canyon, Rocky Point, Garrapato Bridge, Soberantes Point, Point Lobos. The finish is at Rio Road in Carmel.

Runners gather at the finish area and are bussed to the start. The course is entirely on US 1. This is the only event that closes US 1 in the Big Sur area, though there are occasional landslides which close the road and require repair. The Big Sur Marathon has had to use an out-and-back course two times.

There are so many beautiful areas to run that BSIM runners often spend an extra day or more in the area. I enjoy conducting one of my Running Retreats in Carmel in both January and April before the race at Lamplighter Inn in Carmel and highly recommend it.

This course has a strict six–hour limit and tends to be about 20 minutes slower than a fairly flat course. There are other distance options.

For more information:

www.bsim.org

Anchorage RunFest

Date: 3rd weekend of August.

Photos by Kevin Hall and Rebecca Coolidge

Run along the sea coast through areas where there are regular animal sightings. This scenic course has lakes, streams, and forests, and you can walk to and from the start by staying at several nearby hotels.

There's an early start (one hour), and the traditional start time is a very civilized 9 am. The route runs briefly through downtown Anchorage and near the point where the streets parted and buildings slid down the hillside during the 1964 earthquake. After a mile you'll enter a recreational trail that goes along the harbor. Half marathoners turn left and run through a beautiful stretch of parkland and forest. Marathoners continue to enjoy the vistas along the water and then up on a plateau with great views of the water, surrounding islands, and nearby mountains past the airport. I have never felt crowded when running the BWLR marathon.

It's mostly a forest environment, through thick woods where on two different years I've seen a mother moose and her baby (not so little). Also sighted in a different section was a huge bull moose, several eagles, numerous other amazing hawks, and smaller animals.

Moose tip: While there have not been any incidents during the BWLR, if a moose runs at you, hide behind a tree. Their eyesight is not good, and they will avoid the tree.

There are many interesting places to visit while you're in the 49th state: Denali National Park, Seward, Homer, and there is great fishing and boating.

Distances:

49K Ultra, Marathon Run/Walk, Marathon Relay, Half Marathon, 5K, 1-Miler, Kids 2K

For more information:

www.anchoragerunfest.org

Missoula Marathon/Half Marathon/5K

Montana

Traditionally mid-July.

Photos by Tom Robertson Photography

Missoula is my choice for a July marathon or half marathon because morning temperatures tend to be quite comfortable for running, and the course is beautiful. You'll find friendly people, an energetic lifestyle, and a scenic setting on the Clark Fork River (so named after Lewis and Clark navigated this river during their trek West). Among other trails, there's a wonderful rail trail along the Clark Fork river on the University side, going both east and west. The nearby Rattlesnake Trails are included in this book.

Both half and full marathon runners are bussed to the start venues. The half course is quite flat. The marathon course starts in Frenchtown and runs through beautiful (flat) ranchland. There is one hill about half a mile long, coming at about the 13-mile mark. Once up, runners are rewarded with a great view of the valley and nearby mountains. Both courses run into Missoula, through cozy neighborhoods, by the University of Montana and finish downtown.

Beer lovers can enjoy a visit to the Big Sky Brewery—my favorite. There is a great variety of restaurants and foodstores (such as the non-profit Good Foods) featuring local produce and products—such as kamut—an ancient strain of wheat that is grown in Montana. The citizens are proud of their area and for good reason.

While in the area, take a day or three to see Glacier National Park and Flathead Lake. Glacier has amazing scenery, great trails, and beautiful lakes and streams.

If you are having trouble getting flights into Missoula, try Spokane, WA, Bozeman, MT, or Billings, MT.

For more information:
www.runwildmissoula.org

Ogden Marathon/Half Marathon

Traditionally the third week in May.

Photos by Mike McBride, GOAL Foundation

After the 2002 Winter Olympics, the non-profit GOAL Foundation was formed to promote community enthusiasm for fitness. Its mission is in the meaning of the acronym: *Get Out And Live.* The Ogden Marathon/Half Marathon is the centerpiece of GOAL's events and has helped thousands to be active and change their lives for the better.

The course is beautiful and fast—many runners set personal records here. The bonfires at the start are welcome due to normally chilly morning temperatures and inspire cozy gathering and conversations. There's a gradual downhill grade during the first four miles, running along a beautiful mountain stream. The road then enters Ogden Valley, which is surrounded by snow-capped peaks. From miles 5-16, the course is gently rolling through ranchland and along a beautiful lake that reflects off the mountains.

There's a gentle but noticeable uphill at mile 14 for half a mile and then the rewarding view of Pineview Reservoir. Miles 16-21 have a really nice downhill grade along a fast-moving stream. Then the route runs through a city park with little ups and mostly downs. At about mile 24, the course becomes flat and finishes in downtown Ogden.

There are a number of great places to visit in the Ogden area. Some like to have a warm-up run on the ancient shore line trail about 500 feet in elevation above Ogden (see the Bonneville Lake Shoreline Trail listing in this book). There are many great state parks and national parks in the region.

Downtown Ogden has a number of good restaurants, a railroad museum in the old train station, Weber State University, and an interesting history and stories that include visits by Al Capone during the Prohibition era.

For more information:

http://www.getoutandlive.org/ogden-marathon-race-week-details/course-details

Deadwood-Mickelson Trail Marathon and Half Marathon

Deadwood, SD | Near Rapid City, SD and Mount Rushmore

Traditionally the first weekend in June.

Photos by Action Sports Images, Mark Coffey

Both the marathon and the half marathon run through the beautiful Black Hills on a packed gravel rail trail. The marathon starts in the village of Rochford and quickly connects with the historic Deadwood Mickelson Trail. The first 13 miles are slightly uphill through forests and ranches. The second half (which is the half marathon course) is almost completely downhill until the last two miles in Deadwood, which are flat. Many personal records are set on the half marathon course.

History: This rail trail was originally a 114-mile railroad built by the predecessor of the Burlington Northern Railroad in 1890-1891 and last operated in 1983. It connected the leading mining centers in the Black Hills (including the goldrush town of Deadwood). The railroad artifacts include four tunnels and more than 100 converted railroad bridges. There are 15 established trailheads spaced along the route. It was the mission of former South Dakota governor George Mickelson to convert the rail line into a recreational trail. Mickelson died in a plane crash in 1993.

There are many interesting historical towns and sights to see in the area: Rapid City, Spearfish, Sturgis, Custer, Mt Rushmore, Little Big Horn, and the Crazy Horse Monument (under construction). The trail is maintained by the South Dakota Game, Fish and Parks Commission. The first segment of the trail was opened in 1991, and the entire route was completed in 1998.

For more information:

http://gfp.sd.gov/state-parks/directory/mickelson-trail/

For race information:

http://www.deadwoodmickelsontrailmarathon.com/

The Marathon to Finish Breast Cancer/26.2 with Donna/13.1 with Donna

Jacksonville Beach, FL

Traditionally held in the middle of February.

Photos by Straley Photography, Barry Rabinowitz, and Michael Kelly

There's a special inspiration received when running in one of Donna's events. Volunteers who support the cause line the course and thank you for making a difference. Women who are undergoing chemo treatments are running one of the races wearing pink wigs. The Jacksonville community supports this event and so do thousands who come from across the US with many foreign runners represented.

The course runs through some of the most scenic areas in the beach communities of Ponte Vedra Beach, Jacksonville Beach, Atlantic Beach, and Neptune Beach. There's a wonderful sense of freedom when running the segment on the hard packed and wide beach. You'll weave through fun beach neighborhoods and the beautiful marshlands of the intercoastal waterway. Finish area is on the

Mayo Clinic campus, which is appropriate. Most of the proceeds go to breast cancer research at this stellar organization.

For more information:

www.breastcancermarathon.com

7 The Trails

7.1 WEST

South and North Kaibab Trail

Grand Canyon, AZ

Location Info

Closest City: Flagstaff, AZ
Closest Airport: Flagstaff/Pulliam (FLG)
Closest Interstate: 40
Coordinates: South Rim Trailhead 36.03.26.10N 112.08.36.94W, North Rim Trailhead 36.13.01.79N 112.03.22.73W
Best Time: April-May, October-November
High Altitude: South Rim 7000 ft, North Rim 8000 ft
Low Altitude: 2400 ft

Attractions:

* Grand Canyon National Park–South Rim has shops, restaurants, and lots of information about the area and geology
* Grand Canyon Skywalk–step over the canyon's rim on the Hualapai Tribe's reservation

Parking & Access: South Kaibab Trail: parking at Grand Canyon National Park, shuttlebus available. North Kaibab Trail: seasonal access for cars (mid-May to mid-October).

Websites:
www.nps.gov/grca/index.htm
www.backpacker.com/trips/arizona/grand-canyon-national-park/grandcanyon-national-park-south-kaibab-trail-to-bright-angel-trail/#bp = 0/img1
www.americansouthwest.net/arizona/grand_canyon/south_kaibab.html

Flagstaff

The Terrain

South: This 6.5- to 7.1-mile (one way) trail follows the top of a ridge to Skeleton Point with a 360-degree view of the canyon. Altitude drop is almost a mile: 4,820 feet. There is drinking water at the start and at the river bottom but not in between. Because of steep terrain, exposure to the sun, and lack of water, the South Kaibab is a tougher route than Bright Angel trail—but it is a more scenic route.

The run-ability of this trail is based on ability and foot traffic. In many places it is dangerous to run. Be safe and hike if you sense any risk—even walking gently will give you a strenuous workout. It usually takes twice as long to hike up as it took to walk down.

There are a number of out-and-back hikes you can take during a two- to five-hour period. Be sure to bring water! There's no water on the South Kaibab Trail until you reach either Bright Angel Campground or Phantom Ranch. Water from pools, streams, or rivers must be treated and filtered or boiled before drinking.

Caution: If you want to go to the Colorado River you should spend the night at the Bright Angel campground or the Phantom Ranch. Reservations are required.

The trailhead of South Kaibab Trail is located off of the Yaki Point Road, which is closed to private vehicles. While you can come in from the Rim Trail, it is suggested that you park at the Grand Canyon National Park and take the shuttle bus to the trailhead.

At 4.4 miles there's a junction with the Tonto Trail which heads west to Indian Garden and has toilet access. About 500 steps past this trail junction, there's an emergency phone (the tipoff). Then the trail drops significantly. At six miles, the River Trail intersects. One half mile and you're at the Colorado River!

Once at the Colorado River, go over Black Bridge and head southwest for 0.3 mile before turning left and crossing back over on Silver Bridge.

Returning to the South Rim

Take the Bright Angel Trail along Garden Creek to the little oasis of Indian Gardens. The final 2.5 miles follow zig-zagging switchbacks up the canyon wall to the South Rim and the Bright Angel Trailhead.

North Rim is similar terrain but less crowded. There are more logistics involved, so read the USPS website and follow appropriate permitting.

Caution: Summer temperatures can soar into the 100s, so always carry water (rangers recommend 2 gallons per day) and start early to beat the midday heat. Also, don't forget it is much easier to descend into the canyon than to climb back up. Expect to spend at least double the time climbing than descending.

To Trailhead

Start: From S. Lake Powell Blvd. and US 89 in Page, AZ, head southwest on US 89. In 81.5 miles, turn right onto AZ 64. In 53 miles, turn right onto S. Entrance Rd. In 2.7 miles, turn left onto Village Loop Dr. In 0.2 mile, bear left at Village Loop Dr. In 0.2 mile, turn right to stay on Village Loop Dr. In 100 feet, turn left to stay on Village Loop Dr. Go 500 feet and park in Lot E at the South Rim Backcountry Information Center. Take a free shuttle bus to the trailhead (check times at Ranger Station).

End: Follow 0.3 mile to parking on right.

Tahoe Flume Trail

Incline Village/Lake Tahoe, NV

Location Info

Closest City: Carson City, NV
Closest Airport: Reno-Tahoe International Airport (RNO)
Closest Interstate: 580
Coordinates: Spooner Lake Trailhead 39.06.21.37N 119.54.57.21W, Bonanza Ranch Trailhead 39.14.02.01N 119.55.48.31W
Best Time: mid-June-mid-October
High Altitude: 8828 ft
Low Altitude: 6320 ft

Attractions:

* Sand Harbor–magnificent unit of Lake Tahoe Nevada State Park with many beaches and panoramic lake views

Parking & Access: Parking available along Highway 28 at Tunnel Creek Café.

Websites:

www.inclinetrails.org/incline-flume-trail-project
parks.nv.gov/parks/sand-harbor/

Carson City

The Terrain

This might be the most spectacularly scenic trail that we have run. It is one of the hike/runs taken during the Galloway Tahoe Retreat in the summer.

History: During the mining boom in Virginia City (1880s) trees were harvested throughout the Tahoe basin. Near the ridgeline above the northeast corner of the lake was a well-engineered flume system. Lumberjacks would cut the trees and have horses drag the logs to the flume. The logs would float down these man-made streams into a tunnel which would dump them out into Washoe Lake on the other side for transportation to Virginia City. The flume trail follows the most dramatic flume which was cut into the mountainside through major rock formations.

Parking and Trail Access

Parking is available along Highway 28 at Tunnel Creek Café. This is next to what used to be the site of the 1960s-era theme park, The Ponderosa Ranch. One of the owners was Dan Blocker who played Hoss on the TV show. Walk around the Tunnel Creek Cafe on the east side of the road and you'll turn right on Tunnel Creek Road, which parallels Highway 28. This is rough asphalt at first but quickly turns into dirt and takes you up the mountain.

Some really fit runners can run up, but I recommend hiking up (60-70 minutes for most of our runners) to save your resources for the run on top. The surface is sandy but secure in most areas. The elevation increase is almost 2,000 feet—so running up is quite tough. The lake is mostly visible going up and down, and the scenery is superb!

You'll pass by the tunnel entrance after about 45-50 minutes. You can find historical information posted here. The trail turns right and heads to the Flume Trail. Another 10-15 minutes and the single track flume trail will intersect on the right. The trail has random planking which was used in the flume construction.

Within a few minutes you will encounter breathtaking views as the mostly level trail runs along a ledge on the side of the mountain. You can see almost all of Lake Tahoe, ringed by the mountains that once formed a volcano. The Tahoe Rim Trail runs near the ridge line all the way around.

The Western States Trail

Squaw Valley, CA

Location Info

Closest City: Sacramento, CA
Closest Airport: Sacramento International Airport (SMF)
Closest Interstate: 80
Coordinates: Squaw Valley Main Parking 39.11.51.67N 120.14.06.01W
Best Time: Summer
High Altitude: 8750 ft
Low Altitude: 6200 ft

Attractions:

* Western States Endurance Run–100 mile ultramarathon in June

Parking & Access: Parking available along Highway 89.

Websites:
wstrail.org/
www.wser.org/

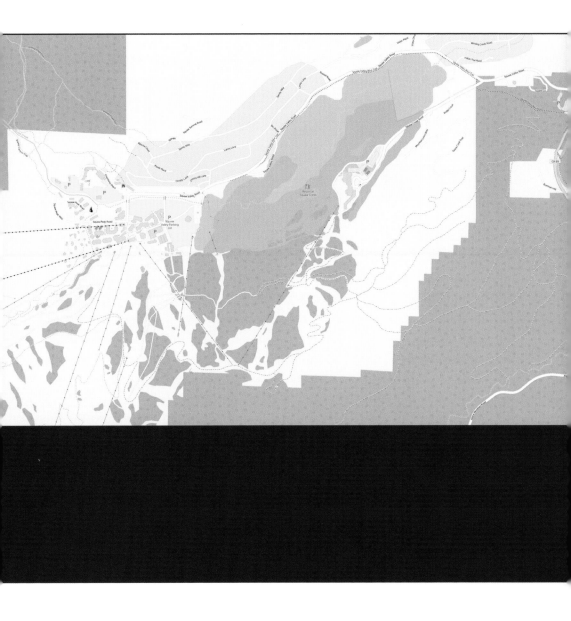

The Terrain

Before roads and railroads, people used trails and travelled by foot. The Western States Trail was a popular way to hike west to Sacramento and then San Francisco. The segment that goes through Squaw Valley became the course for a 100-mile horse race and, later, a 100-mile foot race from Squaw Valley to Auburn, CA. The section described and pictured here starts from Highway 89 where the Truckee River crosses under a bridge, about half a mile south of the entrance to Squaw Valley. There is a paved rail trail (with a connection to the highway bridge) along the Truckee river from Squaw Valley to Tahoe City Trail.

This is one of the trails we run during our Squaw Valley running retreat in the summer and is a scenic journey through the various environments of the Sierra. Parts are too rocky to run, so be aware and walk through these. Those with weak ankles or foot problems should not take this trail. At the north side of this bridge over the west side of the Truckee is the start of this segment of the single track trail. It is marked with a "Western States Trail" sign and takes a short switch back, heading into the woods. There are trail markers but they may be difficult to find. Generally, the trail heads west and uphill on a single track. At the top you will get the first of many spectacular views of Squaw Valley. Use the double-track road that heads down into Squaw Valley. Watch the rocks because they can cause slipping and falling.

After about half a mile, take the first trail to the left. It winds along the side of the mountain for about a mile with amazing views of the valley before intersecting a double track. Turn left for about 100 yards and turn right on another double-track dirt road which will lead down into Squaw Valley to the entrance of the ski area—which is the start of Western States 100-mile running event. Take a walk through the shops in the adjacent village, and head east to the recreation trail along the main road, which will take you to

Highway 89. Cross the road at the stoplight and turn right on the recreation trail which will take you back to the bridge over the Truckee River where this trail began.

Parking and Trail Access
Parking is available along Highway 89 in various places. On the south side near the bridge.

Pacific Crest Trail (PCT)

Segment From Donner Summit Area to Squaw Valley, CA

Location Info

Closest City: Truckee, CA
Closest Airport: Truckee Tahoe Airport (TRK)
Closest Interstate: 80
Coordinates: Old Donner summit rd Trailhead 38.18.52.99N 120.19.37.99W
Best Time: June-October
High Altitude: 9377 ft
Low Altitude: 6906 ft

Attractions:

* Donner Memorial State Park and Emigrant Trail Museum, Truckee
* Squaw Valley Resort/Village–Arial tram, mountaintop swimming and roller skating
* Emerald Bay/Vikingsholm–A historic mansion on the shore of Lake Tahoe with views of the only island in Lake Tahoe and crystal clear water
* Area casinos

Parking & Access: Small parking lot near Donner Pass Road (exit Soda Springs Interstate 80).

Websites:
www.pcta.org/
www.parks.ca.gov/?page_id = 503
vikingsholm.com/

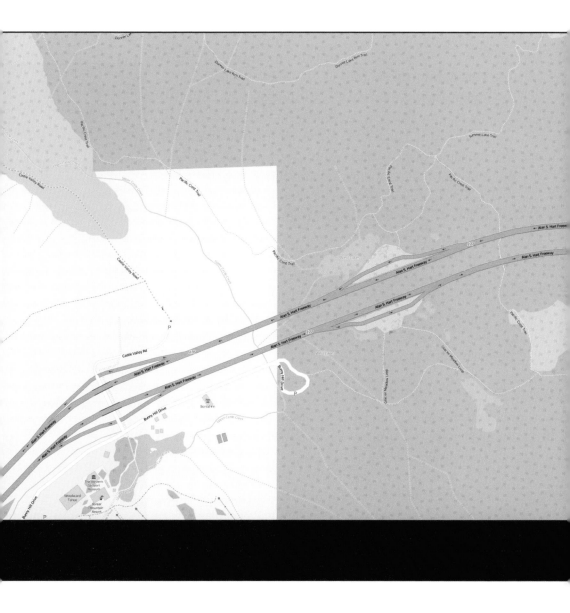

The Terrain

During our summer running retreat at Squaw Valley, CA, we offer this as an optional run/walk of 15 miles on the PCT segment from near Donner Pass into Squaw Valley.

The **Pacific Crest Trail** is a 2,663-mile pedestrian/equestrian trail from the Mexican border to the Canadian border—the pacific coast equivalent of the Appalachian Trail. This is a high-altitude trek for trail veterans but is runnable in most places—but watch terrain carefully. Even into the summer months there can be snow covering the path. Going with someone who knows the trail is the best plan.

Parking and Trail Access

Take the Soda Springs exit off Interstate 80 continue on Donner Pass Road for just over 3.5 miles, turning right and then left where you'll find a small parking lot. Park and follow the path to the trailhead, which is marked with an arrow.

A bit more than a mile later, look for an historical marker where the pioneers hoisted their wagons up a significant and steep grade. This is Roller Pass, so named from a quote by Nicholas Carriger, on Sept. 22, 1846: "We made a roller and fasened (sic) chains to gether (sic) and pulled the wagons up withe (sic) 12 yoke oxen on the top and the same at the bottom." Nicholas was a member of the Donner Party.

Within a mile of generally gentle climbing on a ridgeline, the trees become fewer and the amazing views begin.

You'll also be aware of the geology. The Tahoe area was formed by volcanic activity—and you're walking through the remains which have their own rugged beauty. But glaciers also passed through here, polishing the bedrock and smoothing out the current environment.

It seems to be a desert, but various wild flowers find a way to survive at various times of the year. One of my favorite native plants is the mule's ear, which seems to thrive on finding small patches of dirt between and on the rocks.

The trail runs up some switchbacks toward Anderson Peak to a fork in the trail where there has been no marker. Take the right fork. The other option goes up to the peak and is hardly runnable.

This two-mile path takes you around the base of the peak through rugged, rocky terrain to Tinker Knob—the highest point on this trail segment (8,949 feet). Next junction is the Coldstream Trail to the left—and back to Truckee (don't take it—stay on the main trail). The PCT then switchbacks down to Royal Gorge where the trail turns right. Enjoy a downslope into a valley of mule's ear plants, followed by a climb of over a mile to the final rocky ridge area where you'll come to a trail intersection and a great view. Ahead is the magnificent Granite Chief Mountain that towers over Squaw Valley. Continuing on the PCT trail to this mountain will add about two miles to the hike. The more popular choice, when Squaw Valley is the destination, is to turn left at the Granite Chief Trail marker, taking the Squaw Valley direction.

The climb down is more than three miles, dropping more than 1,500 feet. It really helps to have done some long hikes with significant downhill in preparation for this trek. Otherwise you will probably experience sore quadriceps. Embrace this as your badge of achievement.

Going down you'll go through patches of forest, bushes, mule's ears, and rocky faces. When on the rocks, there are no trail markers—but just keep moving in the direction of Squaw Valley, which you can see below.

You'll make your way to beautiful Squaw Creek, turn left, and take a scenic trail past Olympic Village (so named because that's where the athletes stayed during the 1960 Olympics). You have arrived in Squaw Valley!

Red Rock Canyon

Near Las Vegas, NV

Location Info

Closest City: Las Vegas, NV
Closest Airport: McCarran International Airport (LAS)
Closest Interstate: 15
Coordinates: Red rock canyon–Las Vegas, NV–Visitor's center 36.08.06.74N 115.25.33.02W
Best Time: October-May
High Altitude: 6000 ft
Low Altitude: 3720 ft

Attractions:

* Bellagio fountains
* World-class restaurants
* Famous casinos

Parking & Access: Fees applied due to maintenance. Suggested parking at White Rock Springs or Willow Springs trailheads.

Websites:

www.blm.gov/nv/st/en/fo/lvfo/blm_programs/blm_special_areas/red_rock_nca.html
www.runninglasvegas.com/
www.redrockcanyonlv.org/
www.friendsofredrockcanyon.org/hiking.php

The Terrain

Only 17 miles away from the Las Vegas Strip, you'll find a natural refuge with 19 different trails that cover more than 30 total miles. This was the first National Conservation Area in the state of Nevada. The geological features of this classic Mojave Desert environment were formed millions of years ago, under a massive ocean that covered most of what is now the Western US. The elevation is about one mile (5,280 + ft).

Directions From The Strip

Take Charleston Boulevard/State Route 159 for approximately 17 miles, and you'll drive right into the park.

Parking and Trail Access

A parking fee applies here—but it's for a good cause (maintenance and upgrades of the trail and facilities). We suggest parking at either the White Rock Springs or Willow Springs trailheads, if running the six-mile White Rock Loop. If running the 11-mile Grand Circle loop, park at the Visitor Center. These are our favorite trails.

(Note: The Canyon closes at 5 p.m. from December through February, with longer hours from March through November.)

Bring water—especially during the hot season. Even in the winter, low humidity will leave you more dehydrated than in more humid climates. Watch your step—rattlesnakes live here.

Races

In March, The Red Rock Canyon Marathon and Half Marathon take place. Camping is available, but reserve early.

Porcupine Creek Trail– To North Dome

Yosemite National Park, CA

Location Info

Closest City: Fresno, CA
Closest Airport: Fresno Yosemite International Airport (FAT)
Closest Interstate: 5
Coordinates: Yosemite, CA 120 Trailhead 37.48.24.23N 119.32.42.98W
Best Time: June-October
High Altitude: 8100 ft
Low Altitude: 7540 ft

Attractions:
* Mono Lake
* Yosemite Village
* Numerous spots for wildlife viewing within the park

Parking & Access: Parking available in the Porcupine Creek lot.

Websites:
www.nps.gov/yose/planyourvisit/index.htm
en.wikipedia.org/wiki/Yosemite_National_Park

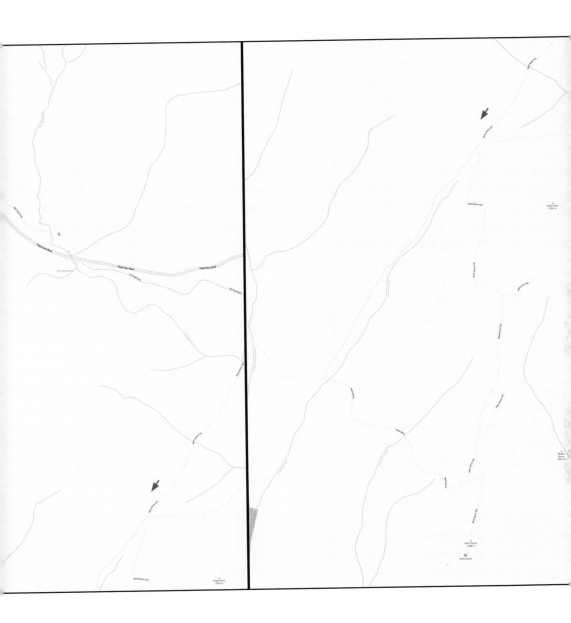

The Terrain

North Dome offers one of the most spectacular views of Yosemite Valley. This eight-plus mile (out and back) trail starts at 8,100 feet altitude and drops down to 7,540 at North Dome—but has significant ups and downs en route. Due to winter challenges the best months are June to November. During the summer there are often streams across the trail. This is a less crowded and less strenuous trail compared with many in Yosemite—but we would not say that it is easy.

The Trail: Generally, this is a runnable trail through meadows and forests. The reward is at the end, on the top of North Dome. A recommended diversion is the Indian Rock loop—featuring a granite arch, about 16 feet high. There are bathrooms at the trailhead. Bring your own food.

Parking and Trail Access
Parking is at the Porcupine Creek lot on Tioga Road (not Porcupine Flat, which is one mile west). From Yosemite Valley, follow signs to Highway 120. Ten miles after leaving the valley, turn right at Crane Flat, then drive 25.5 miles east on Tioga Road. Park in the Porcupine Creek lot.

From the east: Porcupine Creek is 22 miles west of the Yosemite entrance.

Catherine's Pass

Salt Lake City, UT

Location Info

Closest City: Salt Lake City, UT
Closest Airport: Salt Lake City International Airport (SLC)
Closest Interstate: 15, 215
Coordinates: Brighton Ski Area Trailhead 40.35.53.32N 111.34.53.51W
Best Time: Spring & summer
High Altitude: 10,220 ft
Low Altitude: 8755 ft

Attractions:
* Lake Catherine
* Sunset Peak

Parking & Access: Trailhead parking lot near Alta, UT.

Websites:
rootsrated.com/salt-lake-city-ut/hiking/catherine-s-pass
www.visitsaltlake.com/listings/Lake-Mary-Catherine-s-Pass-Trail-Hike/65920/

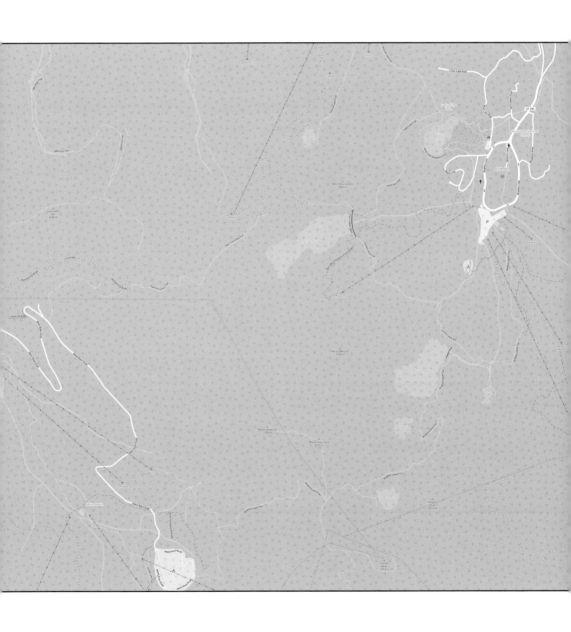

The Terrain

This 1.5-mile trail (one way) is easy to get to, offers great views and scenery, and gets better as you go. Great views of Lake Catherine and Sunset Peak await you at the top of the pass. Running to the top of Sunset Peak is only another mile and is well worth it.

The surface is usually secure and runnable. The incline is gradual—even the extension to Sunset Peak. From the top of the pass, the Sunset Peak trail turns right and has one relatively short and steeper segment near the end where there are three paths to the top. Hint: The one on the right is longer. At the top you'll have a great view of Park City, Big and Little Cottonwood Canyons, Brighton Lakes, Lake Catherine, part of the Salt Lake Valley, and the Heber Valley.

Parking and Trail Access

This trail is located south of Salt Lake City. Take Interstate 15 to Interstate 215 and go East. Take the 6200 South exit. Turn right onto Wasatch Boulevard (209). This road will become Little Cottonwood Canyon Road (210) and lead to the town of Alta, UT. At the east end guard station, use the gravel road to the trailhead parking lot where there is a restroom.

If you are in a party with multiple cars, you may be asked to park unnecessary vehicles and ride up in one or two cars as parking at the trailhead is extremely limited. There is a small parking area just past the guard station for extra cars. Follow the gravel road until you reach the parking area. Remember to park courteously so as to leave room for others to park. There are restroom facilities at the parking area. The trailhead begins across the gravel road to the east. (Lat: 40.58285, Lon:-111.61854)

The Bonneville Lake Shoreline Trail

Salt Lake City, UT

Location Info

Closest City: Salt Lake City, UT
Closest Airport: Salt Lake City International Airport (SLC)
Closest Interstate: 15, 215
Coordinates: University of Utah MC Trailhead 40.46.27.78N 111.50.16.01W
Best Time: June-October
High Altitude: 5200 ft
Low Altitude: 5100 ft

Attractions:

* Park city village
* The great salt lake
* Utah salt flats

Parking & Access: Access via numerous trailheads along the Wasatch Range.

Websites:
www.bonnevilleshorelinetrail.org/index.htm

The Terrain

his trail follows the ancient shoreline of Lake Bonneville—the predecessor of the Great Salt Lake. There are currently 12 segments which run for 100 miles, with plans to extend to 280 miles. Numerous trailheads give access to this trail along the Wasatch Range—with great views of the lake and the great basin.

More than 15,500 years ago, during the Pleistocene period, ancient Lake Bonneville covered much of the western third of the US. This trail follows the eastern shore of this massive lake, at about its highest level, almost 500 feet deeper than today. One would think that because water seeks its own level, this trail would be flat. But there are ravines and stream cuts that required trail makers to adjust up and down, regularly. The trail also follows an active fault: the Wasatch fault as noted by escarpments along the trail.

These pictures were taken from Dry Creek Trailhead segment, near the University of Utah in Salt Lake City.

The Alaska Basin Trail

Grand Teton National Park | Near Alta, WY and Driggs, ID

Location Info

Closest City: Idaho Falls, ID
Closest Airport: Idaho Falls Regional Airport (IDA), Jackson Hole Airport (JAC)
Closest Interstate: 15, 80
Coordinates: Driggs, ID–Trailhead 43.45.20.82N 110.54.44.46W
Best Time: Spring-early summer
High Altitude: 10800 ft
Low Altitude: 7800 ft

Attractions:

* Devil's Stairs

Parking & Access: Access to trailhead via Teton Canyon Road near Alta, WY.

Websites:

www.greater-yellowstone.com/Teton-Valley/South-Teton-Canyon.html

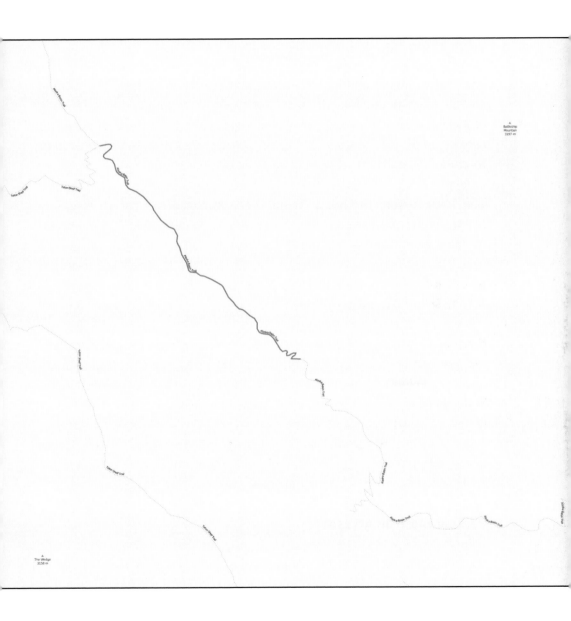

The Terrain

Running through conifer forests, alpine lakes, and meadows, this glacial valley trail is surrounded by snow-capped peaks with abundant wildlife (including bears). The tundra-like terrain inspired the name. The surface is generally runnable, but use caution as in all trail running.

Since this is an out-and-back trail, you may choose the distance by turning around at any point. Total distance one way is seven miles with an upgrade of 2,630 feet. If you plan to spend the night, get a backcountry permit. Be sure to put all food and scented items in bear canisters. Read up on a plan of action (or inaction) when encountering these creatures.

The Route: From the South Teton Creek trailhead the terrain is easier. In the spring and early summer there will be waterfalls and wildflowers. At about 2.7 miles is a sign for an add-on hike to Devil's Stairs. During the next 5 miles to Alaska Basin you'll climb to 9,500 feet. You'll see rock that was polished by the giant glaciers, some small lakes, and only a few trees, but the solitude is amazing.

Caution: Expect snow during any month. The temperature can rise as high as 80° F during the summer. When the sun goes down, the temperature drops quickly, and lows are in the 30s at night. There are occasional thunderstorms in the summer, so take cover. Again, bears live here.

Teton Canyon Campground is a good place to stay because it is adjacent to the South Teton Canyon and Table Mountain trailheads. There are also "bushwhack campsites" along the creek.

Parking and Trail Access

From Jackson, WY: Go to Driggs, ID, turning onto Ski Hill Road. Go through the village of Alta, WY, for about a mile and then turn right on Teton Canyon Road. Pass over two single-lane bridges and look immediately for the trailhead.

Jenny Lake Trail

Grand Teton National Park

Location Info

Closest City: Jackson, WY
Closest Airport: Jackson Hole Airport (JAC), Idaho Falls Regional Airport (IDA)
Closest Interstate: 15, 80
Coordinates: Jenny Lake Visitor's Center 43.45.07.09N 110.43.09.78W
Best Time: June-September
High Altitude: 7100 ft
Low Altitude: 6800 ft

Attractions:

* Jackson, WY town center
* Yellowstone National Park

Parking & Access: Boat dock parking area near Moose Junction.

Websites:

www.tetonhikingtrails.com/jenny-lake.htm

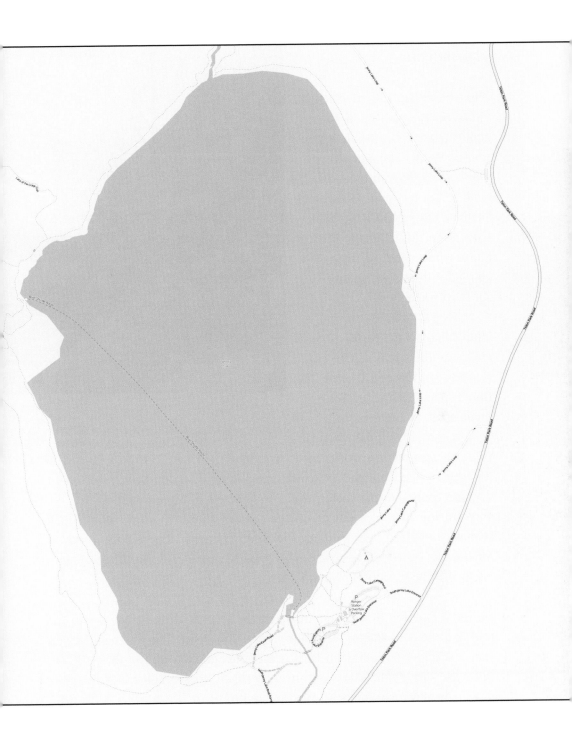

The Terrain

This is a day trip with spectacular views, crossing glacial moraines, alpine meadows, and pine and fir forests. You will be amazed with views of Disappointment Peak, Grand Teton, and Teewinot. Surprise Lake and Amphitheater Lake sit in this dramatic setting above timberline, with a few gnarled trees struggling to survive on the slopes.

Named for a Shoshone Indian who helped an early survey group in the area, Jenny Lake is the second largest lake in the Grand Teton Range and one of the deepest (423 feet).

You can either take the boat shuttle across the lake or run the loop around the lake (7.5 miles). If you run the loop, we recommend the counterclockwise direction because of better sunlight angles. At the visitor center you can get more information.

From the east boat dock, run the eastern shore of Jenny Lake, which is mostly forested with minimal elevation changes. You can see vistas of Mt. Owen, Cascade Canyon, Storm Point, Symmetry Spire, Mt. St. John, Rockchuck Peak, and Mt. Moran.

On the other side of the lake, just past the west boat dock, you'll join the trail that leads to Hidden Falls and Inspiration Point. The Cascade Canyon trail that goes above Hidden Falls is the most popular trail in the park. On the back side of the lake you are more likely to see bears and moose—especially at Moose Ponds (around 6.5 miles).

Parking and Trail Access

Turn west off Teton Park Road at the South Jenny Lake Junction, located roughly 7.7 miles north of Moose Junction. From the junction drive another half-mile to the boat dock parking area.

Hyalite Canyon Trails

Bozeman, MT

Location Info

Closest City: Bozeman, MT

Closest Airport: Bozeman Yellowstone International Airport (BZN)

Closest Interstate: 90

Coordinates: Emerald Lake Trail 45.27.27.68N 11.55.04.03W, Hyalite Reservoir Main Parking Lot 45.29.04.64N 110.58.43.25W

Best Time: June-September

High Altitude: 9000 ft

Low Altitude: 6700 ft

Attractions:

* Yellowstone National Park
* Museum of the Rockies at Montana State University

Parking & Access: Hyalite Canyon Road: national forest parking lot.

Websites:

www.greater-yellowstone.com/Bozeman-MT/Hyalite-Canyon.html

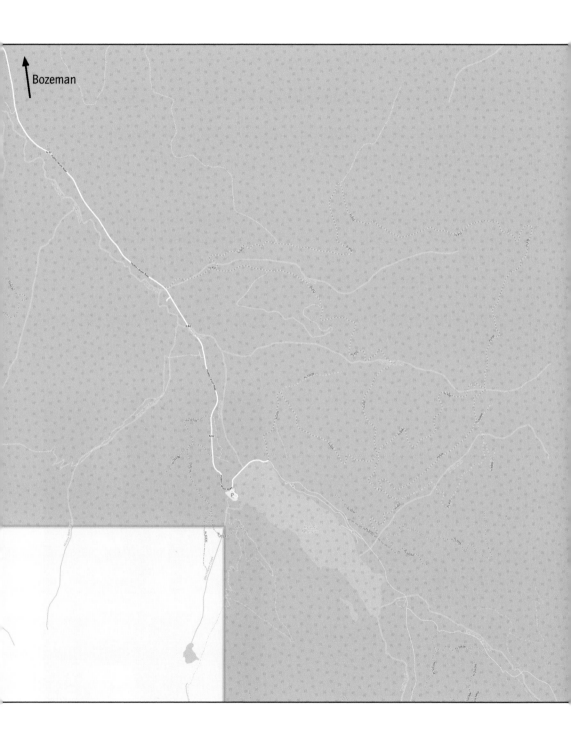

Bozeman

The Terrain

Hyalite Canyon is ringed by snow-capped, 10,000-foot mountains most of the year. Scenic views are everywhere: waterfalls, streams, lakes, and trails. Be aware that hikers often bring their dogs, unleashed. On the hikes to various peaks, the trail at the top may be covered in snow until mid-July. Most trails are out and backs.

History: Giant glaciers sculpted this valley during the ice age. The reservoir was built in the 1940s and inspired local outdoor groups to take advantage of the amazing natural beauty. It is now recognized as the most popular National Forest recreation area in Montana.

Trails: To Blackmore Lake, Palisade Falls, and Emerald and Heather take the trail to Hyalite Lake.

Waterfalls: Grotto Falls, Arch Falls, Champaign Falls, Apex Falls, Silken Skein Falls

Trailheads: History Rock Trailhead is one mile before the reservoir.

Mt Blackmore Trail: Park at the Hyalite Reservoir. Warning: there's a 3,800-foot elevation gain in 5 miles, 10 miles round trip to Mt Blackmore (10,100 feet).

There are lots of areas to run around the beautiful reservoir.

Rattlesnake National Recreation Area

Missoula, MT

Location Info

Closest City: Missoula, MT
Closest Airport: Missoula International Airport (MSO)
Closest Interstate: 90
Coordinates: Missoula, MT 46.55.31.49N 113.50.40.23W
Best Time: June-September
High Altitude: 8600 ft
Low Altitude: 3600 ft

Attractions:

* University of Montana
* Downtown Shopping and Dining District
* Downtown Riverfront

Parking & Access: Parking available at the trailhead.

Websites:

www.makeitmissoula.com/2012/08/missoula-day-hikes-rattlesnakenational-recreation-area/

mountainbiketrailsusa.com/trails/rattlesnake-trail-system-missoulamontana/

mountainbikingmissoula.com/MISSOULA_AREA_TRAIL_MAPS

The Terrain

There are eight trailheads in and around Rattlesnake National Recreation Area, which is part of the Lolo National Forest. Within a few minutes of downtown Missoula you can be running in the Montana forest along Rattlesnake Creek. Look for the orchids.

Parking and Trail Access

From downtown Missoula, follow Van Buren Street north. The name changes to Rattlesnake Drive. Just over four miles from downtown, turn left on Sawmill Gulch Road, cross over the creek, and go about a quarter of a mile to the trailhead and parking.

Coeur d'Alene Lakefront Trail

Coeur d'Alene, ID

Location Info

Closest City: Spokane, WA
Closest Airport: Spokane International Airport (GEG)
Closest Interstate: 90
Coordinates: College Area Trail Access 47.40.44.93N 116.47.42.68W, Higgens Point Trail Access 47.37.45.67N 116.41.04.44W
Best Time: April-October
High Altitude: 2200 ft
Low Altitude: 2100 ft

Attractions:
* Coeur d'Alene Lake Boating
* Silverwood Theme Park

Parking & Access: Parking available at City Park and Beach.

Websites:
friendsofcdatrails.org/CdA_Trail/index.html#.VEf2d8mPu0w

The Terrain

This is a 72-mile paved rail trail has beautiful vistas of lakes, rivers, forests, and mountains. It runs through 13 towns and lots of natural terrain. There are numerous access points near Interstate 90. The section featured here runs along the lake in downtown Coeur d'Alene.

History: The Union Pacific Railroad used this right of way to efficiently haul freight during the heavy mining days in the area. But the Coeur d'Alene Indians had used essentially the same route in their travels.

The trail has become a solution to an environmental problem. Starting in the late 1800s, the residue and waste of the mine, including heavy medals, was used in the rock foundation for the rail line. Spillage during ore shipment contaminated the rail bed further.

The Railroad, the US Government, State of Idaho, and the Coeur d'Alene Tribe worked together to make the area safe by laying thick layer of asphalt with gravel barriers on each side.

From the City Park and Beach, you can access the trail and go in either direction. Much of this section is along the lake, but some miles are through neighborhoods.

Parking and Trail Access

From Interstate 90, take Exit 15. Turn left at the underpass onto Sherman. Go about two miles and park at City Park and Beach.

Cougar Mountain

Seattle, WA

Location Info

Closest City: Seattle, WA
Closest Airport: Seattle-Tacoma International Airport (SEA)
Closest Interstate: 90
Coordinates: Coal Creek Trailhead 47.32.05.08N 122.07.43.78W
Best Time: March-November
High Altitude: 1500 ft
Low Altitude: 500 ft

Attractions:
* Space Needle
* Pike Place Market

Parking & Access: Various parking lots available at Cougar Mountain, e.g. Sky Country Trailhead.

Websites:
your.kingcounty.gov/ftp/gis/Web/VMC/recreation/BCT_CougarMtn_brochure.pdf

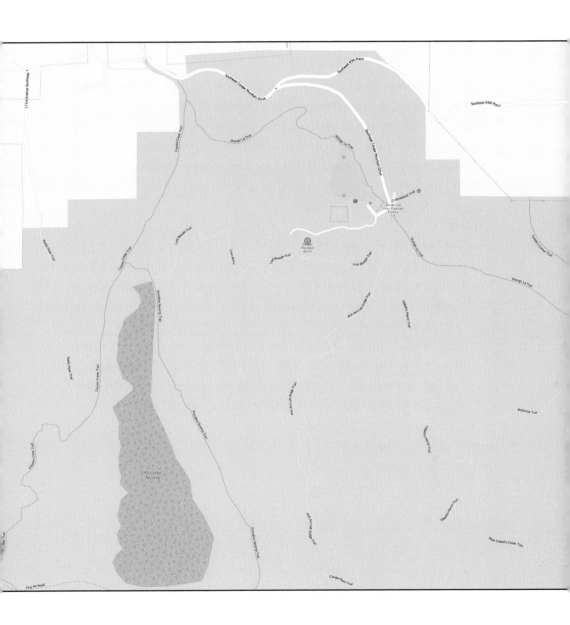

The Terrain

Cougar Mountain has 36 delightful miles of running/hiking trails in various loops. You'll see natural flora and fauna and run through what was the first industrial area in Seattle and a vibrant mining community for about 100 years.

In 1863, coal was discovered on Cougar Mountain and provided Seattle with a vibrant industry. Tunnels were first installed six miles deep, and a railroad line was built from the mine to the docks. In later years surface mining or strip mining was used to keep the mine operating for about 100 years. After years of decay and abandonment, conservationists were able to have the county designate Cougar Mountain as a park.

Trails

* Red Town Loop: So called because the Pacific Coast Coal Company painted all the buildings red. From the parking lot, turn left on Red Town Trail, and you will begin a tour of collapsed mine shafts, debris, and random pieces of mining equipment over what used to be a town of 50 houses, hotel, and stores.
* Coal Creek Trail: Trailhead is across Lakemont Blvd from the Red Town Parking lot. The three-mile (one way) trail goes past the remains of the railroad, the coal loading building, bridges, and waterfall (in winter), the remains of Newcastle School, and other interesting sights.

Point Defiance Park Trails

Tacoma, WA

Location Info

Closest City: Tacoma, WA

Closest Airport: Seattle-Tacoma International Airport (SEA)

Closest Interstate: 705

Coordinates: Tacoma, WA–Five mile road entrance 47.18.06.89N 122.30.58.08W

Best Time: March-November

High Altitude: 300 ft

Low Altitude: 100 ft

Attractions:

* Point Defiance Zoo
* Mount Rainier
* Tacoma Museum District

Parking & Access: Parking lot: 5400 N. Pearl St, Tacoma, WA 98407.

Websites:

www.metroparkstacoma.org/five-mile-drive

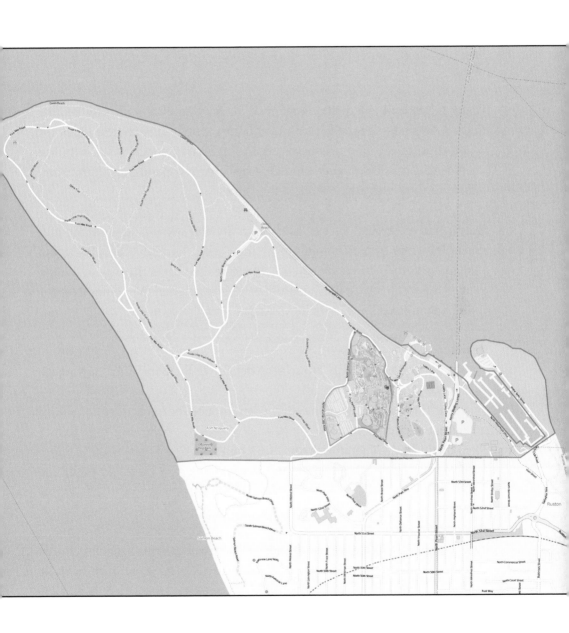

The Terrain

Only minutes from Interstate 5, you can run along cliffs overlooking Puget Sound where bald eagles soar and feed on salmon during the spawning season. On the north end you'll find an old growth forest. Wildlife sightings include sea lions, harbor seals, mule deer, fox, squirrel, raccoon, and many birds.

History: The Wilkes Expedition mapped the bays and waterways of the area in the 1840s and suggested that the cliff area would be a strategic area for a fort—but the location was never used for military operations. About forty years later, President Grover Cleveland declared it a public park, and soon streetcars were bringing visitors to the gardens.

Even prior to Wilkes' survey operation, Hudson's Bay Company brought goods from the British Empire and traded with the native people. In the park today you'll find Fort Nisqually, which is a replica of the type of trading centers the company established from Fort Vancouver on the Columbia River to the Yukon River in what is now Alaska.

Trails
* Square Trail is generally around the outside of the park and is just under 5 miles.
* Spine Trail is 1.3 miles (one way) from Rhododendron Garden to the Gig Harbor overlook.
* Triangle Trail—The inner loops is 3.3 miles.
* Five Mile Drive (the road around the park) is also closed to traffic for pedestrian use on Saturday and Sunday until 1 pm.

Parking and Trail Access
Take Interstate 705 north to Schuster Parkway which becomes North Waterview Street, then Ruston Way, and finally N 51st Street. Turn right on N Pearl. Drive into the park to parking lot: 5400 N. Pearl St, Tacoma, WA 98407.

Portland's Forest Park

Portland, OR

Location Info

Closest City: Portland, OR
Closest Airport: Portland International Airport (PDX)
Closest Interstate: 5, 405
Coordinates: Wildwood Trail NW Cornell Rd Trailhead 45.31.36.60N 112.43.35.51W
Best Time: March-November
High Altitude: 1100 ft
Low Altitude: 50 ft

Attractions:
* Portland Saturday Market
* Powell's City of Books
* Voodoo Doughnut

Parking & Access: Parking available on NW Cornell Road.

Websites:
www.forestparkconservancy.org/forest-park/maps/
www.portlandoregon.gov/parks/42336

The Terrain

This park is amazing. Only a few minutes from downtown Portland, but you're running on trails in the Oregon woods. There are more than 152 miles of trails, with a minority of the segments on fire lanes and forest roads. Most of the trails are easily runnable, with the usual caution of looking for random branches or rocks.

Touted as the largest urban park in the US, Forest Park extends more than seven miles with great vistas of the Willamette River, downtown Portland, and occasionally, Mt. Hood.

The Wildwood Trail is our favorite. Once you reach the ridgeline on runnable switchbacks, there are very few significant ups or downs. It is marked every. 25 mile by diamond shapes on the trees and is more than 30 miles long (one way).

Leif Erikson Drive was once a city street that has been converted into a scenic forest trail (only in Oregon!). It's more than 11 miles long, and you can access it from the NW Thurman Street trailhead, or the other end at NW Germantown Road.

Maple Trail Loop (just over 6 miles both ways): For running variety, you can't beat this one: authentic trails, a few steep uphills, gently paved inclines and a fun downhill rolling segment along a creek. Access at Saltzman Road off Highway 30, right at Maple Trail sign, go left on Leif Erikson, and left on the Maple Trail to take you back to the start.

Lithia Park

Ashland, OR

Location Info

Closest City: Ashland, OR
Closest Airport: Rogue Valley International-Medford Airport (MFR)
Closest Interstate: 5
Coordinates: Ashland, OR 42.10.41.67N 122.43.05.87W
Best Time: April-October
High Altitude: 6500 ft
Low Altitude: 1900 ft

Attractions:
* Rogue River Rafting
* Local Wineries

Parking & Access: Various parking lots available at Lithia Park.

Websites:
ashland.or.us/Files/BandersnatchAccess.pdf
www.ashland.or.us/Files/WhiteRabbit.pdf
www.ashland.or.us/Files/FourCorners.pdf
www.ashland.or.us/Files/Lithia_Loop.pdf
www.ashland.or.us/Page.asp?NavID = 11458

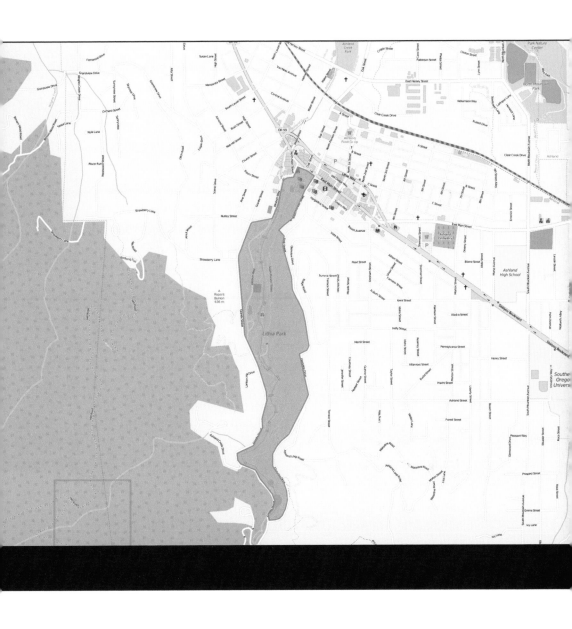

The Terrain

On the site of what was once a flour mill along Ashand Creek is the largest park in Ashland. You can run on four trails in this canyon that stretch from downtown to the creek's origin at Mt. Ashland. Lithium oxide, or "lithia," was discovered in the stream water in the area and sparked hopes for a health resort. Today, runners and walkers use the trails all day long—creating their own health resort.

History: Abel Helman and Eber Emery established a flour mill in 1852, and the town of Ashland Mills grew up around it. By 1900 the mill was in ruins and the property run-down. An active Chautauqua group in Ashland lobbied the city government to improve cultural activities and upgrade the quality of life by creating a park on the mill site. An elected park commission was established and designated the city land along Ashland Creek as a park.

In 1907, in a nearby stream (Emigrant Creek), lithium oxide was discovered in almost the same levels as advertised by the health resort town of Saratoga, NY. A movement developed to establish a mineral springs resort in Ashland, and in 1914 the designer of Golden Gate Park in San Francisco was hired to design the park. Lithia water was piped from Emigrant Creek into Ashland Creek, and Lithia Park was born. The resort never really took off, and the park was developed for recreational pursuits.

Four trails run through the park:
* Bandersnatch and BTI trails
* White Rabbit and Caterpillar Trail, Siskiyou Mtn Park, Lamb Saddle
* Lamb Saddle, Toothpick, Catwalk, Four Corners
* Lithia Loop Trail

Marin County Coastal Trail

Marin County, CA

Location Info

Closest City: San Francisco, CA
Closest Airport: San Francisco International Airport (SFO)
Closest Interstate: 580
Coordinates: Tennessee Valley Trailhead 37.51.37.54N 122.32.10.57W
Best Time: Year-round
High Altitude: 1000 ft
Low Altitude: 0 ft

Attractions:

* Golden Gate Bridge
* Muir Woods
* San Francisco Presidio

Parking & Access: Parking available e.g. at Rodeo Beach.

Websites:

www.californiacoastaltrail.info/hikers/hikers_main.php?DisplayAction = DisplayCounty&CountyId = 6
www.parks.ca.gov/?page_id = 471
www.nps.gov/nps/pore/index.htm

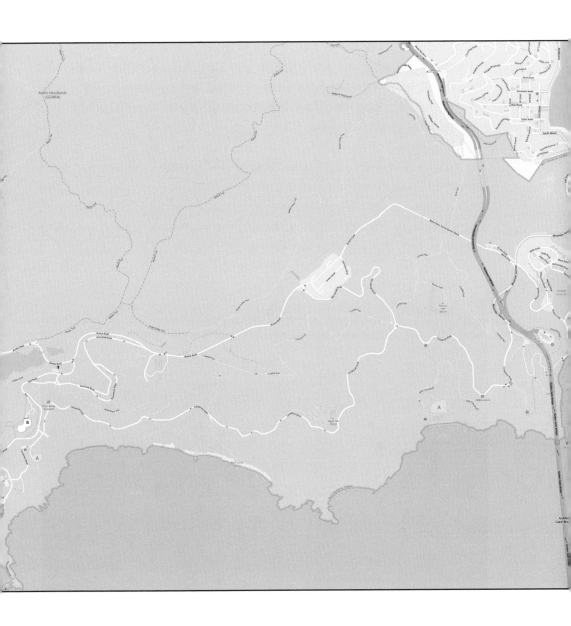

The Terrain

Because of focused lobbying by local citizens in the 1960s and 1970s, a huge section of prime Pacific coast land was set aside—over 140,000 acres. The San Andreas fault passes through this land. There are hundreds of miles of trails starting on the north side of the Golden Gate Bridge to Point Reyes National Park. The trails through Pt Reves, Mt Tamapais, Muir Woods, and the Golden Gate National Recreation Area are not surpassed by any trail system we have found. The vistas are amazing, and the natural beauty leads you on, one segment at a time.

The coastal trail itself is 60 miles long. Jeff's favorite is the section from Bolinas to Point Reyes where you'll not only enjoy ocean views, but weave among lakes, on top of cliffs, along cozy beaches, through oaks, evergreens, and native sage. Wildlife is seen often except for poisonous snakes. According to experts, they don't live on the western (ocean side) of the fault.

Colorado Trail

Kenosha Pass, CO

Location Info

Closest City: Denver, CO
Closest Airport: Denver International Airport (DEN)
Closest Interstate: 70
Coordinates: Waterton Canyon (Eastern Terminus near Denver) 39.29.25.46N 105.05.48.14W, Kenosha Pass (Hwy 285) 39.24.45.52N 105.45.30.16W
Best Time: April-October
High Altitude: 13,271 ft
Low Altitude: 5520 ft

Attractions:
* 16th Street Dining & Shopping (Denver)
* Mining Town of Leadville
* Durango and Silverton Narrow Gauge Railroad &Museum (Durango)

Parking & Access: Various access points along the trail, not all accessible for passenger cars.

Websites:
funcoloradohikes.com/kenosha_pass.html#sthash.eJ09eJF2.dpuf
americantrails.org/resources/statetrails/COstate.html
www.coloradotrail.org/faq.html

The Terrain

The 500-mile Colorado Trail connects Denver with Durango through some amazing Rocky Mountain scenery. The average elevation is 10,000 feet, but the path has constant ups and downs, totaling almost 90,000 feet of climbing.

Kenosha Pass segment is only one of the many day runs that are accessible from highways. This trail begins just off of Highway 285 at Kenosha Pass campground. There is no restroom in the parking lot. Mostly runnable, you'll pass through pine and aspen forests for about two miles. Great vistas open up at this point—looking at a huge valley toward South Park and Fairplay, CO. During the warm months there are alpine flowers, butterflies, and great views.

Another recommended Colorado Trail segment is the Twin Lakes loop near Leadville.

Barr Trail

Colorado Springs, CO

Location Info

Closest City: Colorado Springs, CO
Closest Airport: Colorado Springs Airport (COS)
Closest Interstate: 25
Coordinates: Colorado Springs, CO 38.51.21.40N 104.56.01.93W
Best Time: Summer
High Altitude: 14118 ft
Low Altitude: 6707 ft

Attractions:
* Cheyenne Mountain Zoo
* Aramark Pikes Peak
* City of Cripple Creek

Parking & Access: Parking lot in Manitou Springs. Free shuttle bus from there to the base of Barr Trail.

Websites:
barrtrail.net/
www.visitcos.com/venue/parks/Barr-Trail-Pikes-Peak

The Terrain

This is the trail used during the Pikes Peak Marathon from Manitou Springs. It gains over 7,000 feet of altitude and tops out at 14,115 feet. It was named for Fred Barr, who loved the mountains and constructed over 100 miles of trails.

History: Fred's father William moved the family (originally from Arkansas) to Colorado Springs when Fred was 11. William developed a burro and tourist transportation business in the area, and when he was 18 (1900) Fred joined him in the business. While he made his living transporting people, Fred's love was the mountains.

During the summer he developed a burro livery service to transport tourists up to Pikes Peak. He built several cabins at about 10,000 feet elevation—and one is still being used. During the winter, when business was slow, he climbed Pike's Peak and started constructing a trail. He was a member of the small and hearty AdAmAn Club whose members climbed Pike's Peak on New Year's Eve and set off fireworks at midnight. Fred spent his life building the trail that is currently used today, using more than $30,000 of his own funds.

The Trail: Starting in Manitou Springs (at over 7,000 feet elevation), the trail heads up the mountain through a forest environment. The incline to the top is steady and constant with many switchbacks. About two-thirds of the trip is above the tree line.

Trailhead: The main trailhead is on Ruxton Street in Manitou Springs.

Information on Fred Barr is thanks to two excellent articles by Eric Swab and Deb Acord. Here are a few of Deb's observations:

"Barr Camp is approximately 6.5 miles from the trail head in Manitou Springs. Elevation gain is 3,800 feet, and the camp elevation is 10,200 feet (3,109 meters). You can expect a 20 degree temperature difference between the bottom of the trail and Barr Camp. Expect changeable weather any time of the year.

Pikes Peak is an additional 6 miles from Barr Camp, and the trail climbs another 3,900 feet to the summit at over 14,000 feet (4,301 meters). Expect another 20 degree change in temperature and extreme weather changes such as high winds, thunderstorms, and snow.

Barr Camp has no potable water. There is a running stream at the camp where you will be able to filter or treat your water. We recommend you bring your own filter or treatment."

Garden of the Gods

1805 N 30th Street, Colorado Springs, CO

Location Info

Closest City: Colorado Springs, CO
Closest Airport: Colorado Springs Airport (COS)
Closest Interstate: 25
Coordinates: Colorado Springs, CO–Kissing Camels Parking Lot 38.52.52.98N 104.52.48.65W
Best Time: April-October
High Altitude: 6600 ft
Low Altitude: 6210 ft

Attractions:
* United States Air Force Academy
* US Olympic Training Center
* The Broadmoor Resort

Parking & Access: Kissing Camels Parking Lot.

Websites:
friendsofgardenofthegods.org/Trails.aspx

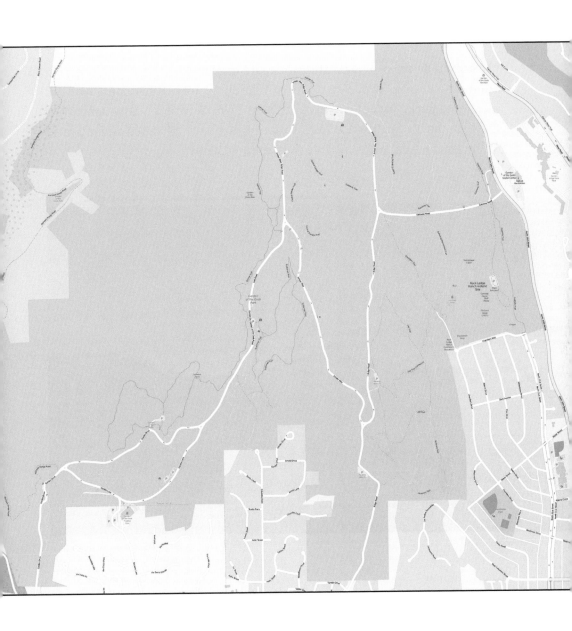

The Terrain

The Garden of the Gods is a National Park with unique geological formations. There are numerous trails that wind through these natural monuments and several historical sites used by native peoples.

History: The major upheaval that created the dramatic landscape occurred millions of years ago. Some of the interesting rock formations, such as Balanced Rock, were put in place during the glacial period. Native Americans were in the area before 1000 BC. Various tribes have inhabited and migrated through the area, believing it to be a spiritual center.

Pino Trail

Albuquerque, NM

Location Info

Closest City: Albuquerque, NM
Closest Airport: Albuquerque International Sunport (ABQ)
Closest Interstate: 25, 40
Coordinates: Albuquerque, NM 35.09.47.81N 106.28.12.81W
Best Time: March-November
High Altitude: 9627 ft
Low Altitude: 6440 ft

Attractions:

* Sandia Peak Tramway
* Balloon Rides (Year-round) and Balloon Festival (October)
* Historic Town of Santa Fe (Short Drive)

Parking & Access: Parking lot at Elena Gallegos Picnic Ground (fee area).

Websites:
www.cabq.gov/parksandrecreation/open-space/lands/elena.pdf

Driving Instructions

From Interstate 40 E take Tramway Blvd. north. Turn Right (east) to Elena Gallegos Picnic Ground and park in lot. This is a fee area.

Hike Description

Pino Trail is one of the most popular trails in the area, going east, up to the ridgeline between Sandia Crest and South Peak. Because of the altitude (6,500 feet at the start and 9,000 to 10,000 feet on top), liberal walk breaks are recommended on the way up. It's an out-and-back hike, so you can turn around at any time. Round-trip distance as described is about eight miles.

History: Sandia Peaks form a stand-alone mountain range uplifted as a fault block within the last 10 million years. It is believed that the first humans came to live in these mountains 10,000 to 12,000 years ago. Sandia means "watermelon" in Spanish. One theory is that the Spanish explorers thought that the native gourds were melons.

Follow the signs for Pino trailhead. About a mile from your car you'll enter a wilderness area, and you should stay east, ascending the southern side of Pino Canyon. Watch your footing for the first two miles; it's a rocky trail. You'll pass through forest environment and will be above the tree line for the last few miles—with a steeper grade.

The round-trip distance up and down Pino Trail is about eight miles.

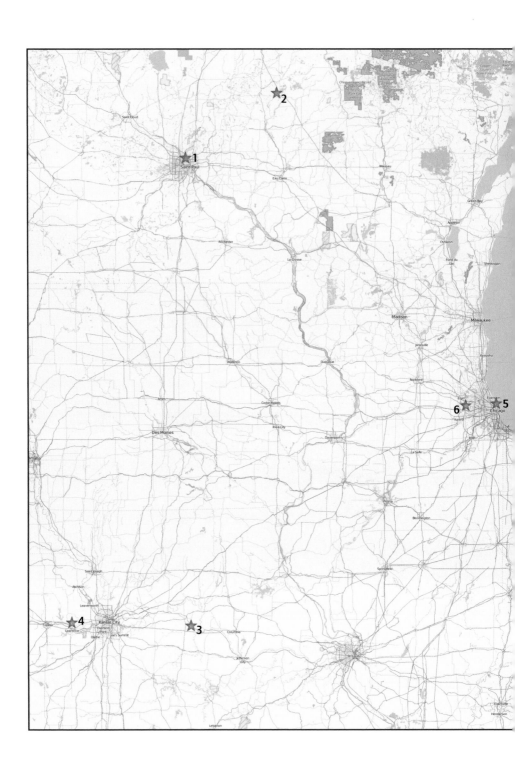

7.2 MIDWEST

Minneapolis Lakes

Minneapolis, MN

Location Info

Closest City: Minneapolis, MN
Closest Airport: Minneapolis-Saint Paul International Airport (MSP)
Closest Interstate: 94
Coordinates: Minneapolis, MN–Lake Harriet Bandshell Parking 44.55.41.42N 93.18.31.08W
Best Time: April-October
High Altitude: 900 ft
Low Altitude: 869 ft

Attractions:
* Sculpture Garden at Walker Arts Center
* Mall Of America
* Nice Ride Bike Sharing (With paths to easily access the city)

Parking & Access: Various parking lots near the lakes available.

Websites:
www.minneapolisparks.org/parks__destinations/parks__lakes/
www.dnr.state.mn.us/minneapolis_iba.html

The Terrain

"Parks are imbued with personal meaning—the playgrounds that live in the memories of generations of people, are the soul of our communities." Minneapolis Park and Recreation Board

In 1883, the voters of Minneapolis voted to establish a park board with independent authority to acquire and manage parks. The vision and development of this park system placed preservation of lakes and rivers as the top priority.

Lake of the Isles, Lake Calhoun, and Lake Harriet

There are many lakes and many trail systems in the Minneapolis/St. Paul area. The following featured lakes have both a bike lane and a pedestrian lane. All three lakes listed are connected in a Scenic Byway so that you can run from one to the other without having to get out on the streets.

Lake of the Isles was a shallow lake and swampy marsh. In the early 1900s it was dredged and sculpted into the beautiful configuration you see today, which is almost three miles around. The dredged material was deposited into low areas with natural landscaping as usable park land. You'll run by two original islands, Mike's Island and Raspberry Island, which are off limits to protect vegetation.

Lake Calhoun has a 3.2-mile run/walk trail around and connects to Lake of the Isles, Lake Harriet, and Cedar Lake in the northeast. There's also a connection to the Midtown Greenway Trail, just north of the lake and just south of Lake Street. This is a special place for the Galloways because Brennan and Jenny Galloway were married in the Calhoun Beach Club.

The first home in Minneapolis was built on the east side of the lake by a missionary, Gideon Pond. The Bakken Museum, which displays the study of electricity in life, is on the west side.

The Dakota named the lake White Earth Lake. Early settlers renamed it "Medoza," which is Dakota for "Loon Lake." But the official name on the first official map was listed by US Army surveyors who named it after their boss, Secretary of War, John C. Calhoun.

Birkie Trail

Hayward, WI

Location Info

Closest City: Minneapolis, MN

Closest Airport: Minneapolis-Saint Paul International Airport (MSP)

Closest Interstate: 35

Coordinates: Hayward, WI–County Hwy. OO Trailhead 46.06.32.83N 91.17.48.13W

Best Time: April-June, September-October

High Altitude: 1750 ft

Low Altitude: 1200 ft

Attractions:
* Boating on the Lakes
* Kayaking/Canoeing the Namekagon River
* Downtown Hayward Shopping, Dining, and Festivals (Lumberjack World Championships, Musky Festival)

Parking & Access: Parking passes for Birkie Trail use not required April till November.

Websites:
www.birkie.com/run/

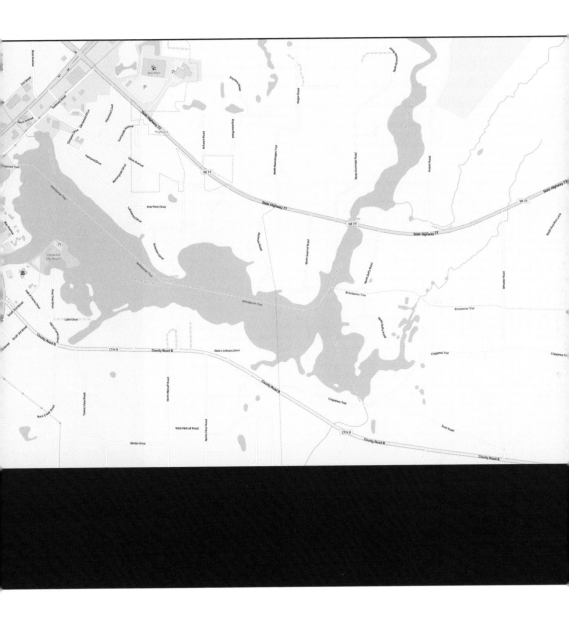

The Terrain

The 67-mile trail was developed as a vision of Wisconsin promoter Tony Wise who started the Telemark Ski Area in 1947 to popularize cross-country skiing. In 1973 he conducted the first long-distance ski race, the Birkiebeiner. This event, held in Norway, commemorates a brave group of soldiers who saved a royal baby by smuggling him and skiing through rough frozen territory to safety. Today the race is capped at 10,000 and attracts skiers from around the world and over 20,000 spectators.

But the cross-country ski trails make good running trails in the warm months. The many hills on the course have colorful names: Bobblehead, Sledder, Bitch, El Moco. There are many scenic segments and none that are flat.

Katy Trail

Columbia, MO

Location Info

Closest City: Columbia, MO; St. Louis, MO
Closest Airport: Columbia Regional Airport (COU), Lambert St. Louis International Airport (STL)
Closest Interstate: 70
Coordinates: Columbia, MO 38° 57' 6.139" N 92° 20' 2.661" W
Best Time: April-November
High Altitude: 955 ft
Low Altitude: 452 ft

Attractions:
* Gateway Arch (St. Louis)
* Cathedral Basilica of St. Louis
* Boonville Historic Districts (Boonville)

Parking & Access: Various parking lots available, e.g. Creve Coeur Park, St. Charles Trailhead.

Websites:
www.bikekatytrail.com/katy-trail-map.aspx

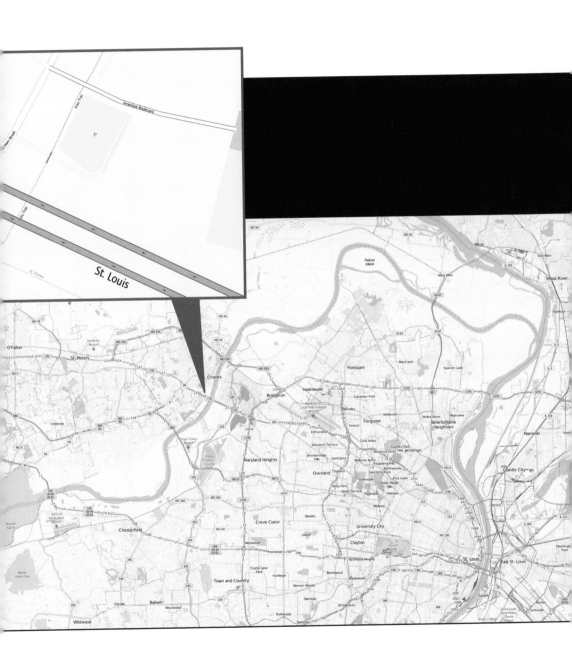

The Terrain

Katy Trail State Park is a 240-mile rail trail, the former corridor of the Missouri-Kansas-Texas (MKT) Railroad (better known as the Katy). The Union Pacific Railroad donated another 33 miles of rail corridor from Sedalia to east of Clinton, and there have been other extensions.

The trail follows the scenic route of the Missouri River, often with the river on one side and steep inclines on the other. It runs through wetlands, valleys, thick forested areas, pastures, and gently rolling terrain. A great variety of wildlife can be seen.

The route passes through a number of towns, including the area known as "Missouri's Rhineland." Emigrants from Germany settled in this area before the Civil War.

Although the scenery often changes, the trail remains fairly level and constant as it meanders through the countryside. Trailheads, which provide parking areas and other amenities, are located periodically along the trail. Many communities also offer services to trail users.

The section of trail between St. Charles and Boonville has been designated as an official segment of the Lewis and Clark National Historic Trail, and the entire trail is part of the American Discovery Trail. The trail also has been designated as a Milennium Legacy Trail.

For more information:
For more information about the trail, call the Department of Natural Resources toll free at 800-334-6946 (voice) or 800-379-2419 (TDD).

Lawrence, KS

Location Info

Closest City: Topeka, KS; Kansas City, MO
Closest Airport: Kansas City International Airport (MCI)
Closest Interstate: 70
Coordinates: Lawrence, KS 38.58.35.22N 95.14.05.80W
Best Time: April-November
High Altitude: 860 ft
Low Altitude: 840 ft

Attractions:

* Massachusetts Street District
* Booth Family Hall of Athletics
* Spencer Museum of Art

Parking & Access: From Interstate 70, exit 204: parking available in Massachusetts Street.

Websites:

lawrenceks.org/lprd/parks

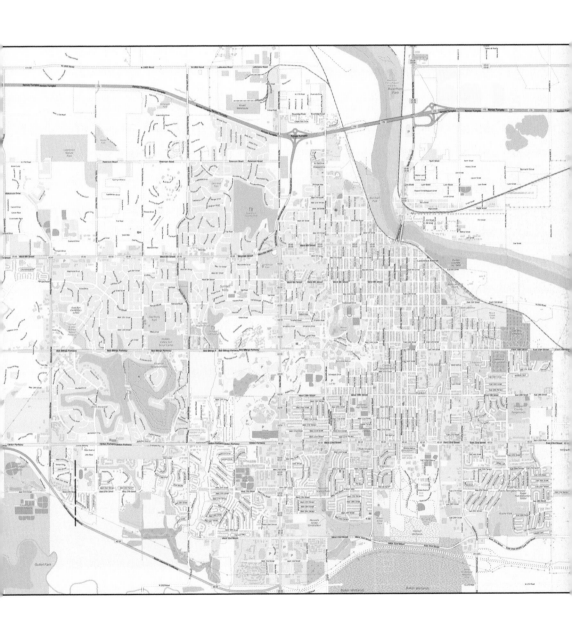

Thanks to J Jenkins for logistics.

Photography by Alex O'Nelio

Legendary runners such as Jim Ryun and Billy Mills ran in Lawrence during their university years. There is a lot of excitement about running here, and you'll see a lot runners every day on the river trail.

Description: Run along the levee on the north side of the Kansas River. On the eastern end of the levee trail is a network of single-track trails with gentle rolling hills.

Parking and Trail Access

From Interstate 70, take exit 204 and head south on N 2nd Street for about 1.2 miles to the bridge over the Kansas river. The street changes to Massachusetts Street.

Option one: Just across the river in Lawrence's historic downtown shopping district is the town's local running store, Ad Astra Running, home to the area's largest collection of running memorabilia as well as the local Galloway training program, RunWalkLawrence. Park anywhere along Massachusetts street and run about a quarter mile north, crossing the Kansas River bridge. Trailhead is on the right.

Option two: Use the parking lot along the levee. From the Massachusetts Street bridge just mentioned, go east on Elm Street (the first street north of the river). Turn right (south) onto 8th Street and park in the lot. The single-track trails are about a mile east on the levee trail.

Lakefront Trail

Chicago, IL

Location Info

Closest City: Chicago, IL
Closest Airport: Chicago O'Hare International Airport (ORD)
Closest Interstate: 55, 90
Coordinates: Millennium Park Access Point 41.52.52.66N 87.37.00.25W
Best Time: April-October
High Altitude: 590 ft
Low Altitude: 577 ft

Attractions:

* Monroe Harbor
* Waveland Clock Tower
* Soldier Field

Parking & Access: Many parking lots available along the trail.

Websites:
www.choosechicago.com/articles/view/the-lakefront-trail/454/
www.navypierflyover.com/

North

South

Photos by Don Williams with Don Shutters

The Chicago Lakefront Trail (abbreviated as LFT) is a beautiful 20-mile pathway along the shore of Lake Michigan, extending north and south. While the route is paved, there are many sections nearby composed of packed gravel or dirt. There are great vistas of the city, the lake, and of the many scenic parks along the way. A growing number of people use this trail to commute.

The trail extends from 7100 South/2560 East to 5800 North/1000 West, all within the city limits. You can run through the great parks of Chicago on this trail: Lincoln Park, Grant Park, Burnham Park, and Jackson Park.

Landmarks along the trail:
* South Shore Country Club
* Museum of Science and Industry
* McCormick Place
* Soldier Field
* Chicago's Museum Campus
* Navy Pier
* Monroe Harbor
* Belmont Harbor
* Waveland Clock Tower
* 3 Skate Parks

Challenges: Most of the trail is traffic-free, but there are a few exceptions. Be aware of possible crossings, especially at the Navy Pier area. During the winter, wave action and cold temperatures expose several areas to ice formation—so be careful (especially at the Oak Street Curve).

The *Active Transportation Alliance* promotes using the **#chiLFT** hashtag on Twitter, so users, especially commuters, can be informed of hazards and warn others.

Parking and Trail Access

Parking is available at nearly all of the parks, on city streets, and at paid parking garages. On sunny days, especially in spring and summer, there are few open free parking spaces.

The Illinois Prairie Path (IPP)

Wheaton, IL

Location Info

Closest City: Wheaton, IL
Closest Airport: Chicago O'Hare International Airport (ORD)
Closest Interstate: 88, 355
Coordinates: Aurora Trailhead 41.46.14.59N 88.18.27.06W, Maywood Trailhead 41.52.35.29N 87.50.02.26W, Wheaton Trailhead 41.51.50.26N 88.06.57.94W, Elgin Trailhead 42.00.47.42N 88.16.27.89W
Best Time: April-November
High Altitude: 815 ft
Low Altitude: 660 ft

Attractions:

* Millennium Park/Navy Pier
* Willis (Sears) Tower Observation Deck
* The Art Institute of Chicago

Parking & Access: Parking available at almost all trailheads.

Websites:
www.ipp.org/trail-maps/

This is one of the first rail trails in the US, following the rail bed of the Chicago, Aurora, and Elgin electric railroad (1902-1959) from the western suburbs to downtown Chicago. There are five trail segments with the three main ones linking at Volunteer Park in Wheaton. Naturalist May Theilgaard Watts started the trail conversion movement with a letter in the Chicago Tribune in 1963.

Main branch:
This 17-mile segment is the most "urban." Green markers will lead you east alongside the Metra commuter rail line and then into one western suburb after another. The trail seems to end at First Avenue in Maywood. Take Maybrook Drive to a pedestrian bridge over the Des Plaines River, continuing to the eastern end at the Forest Park CTA Station. Don't count on free parking at this end of the trail.

Aurora branch:
Beginning at the Fox River Trail in Aurora, this 13-mile segment along Aurora Branch heads north through a commercial/older neighborhood mix on a strip of asphalt. After one mile, the surface changes to a hard-packed crushed stone and angles northwest, away from the river. The IPPs Batavia Branch connects five miles later, leading to the namesake town (6 miles). Wildlife can be seen along the Aurora trail through woods and fields. At about mile 7, at Winfield Road, other trails converge. Look for the green IPP marker across Winfield Road.

Elgin branch:

This 14-mile branch between Elgin and Volunteer Park in Wheaton has a hard-packed dirt/rock surface. From Elgin at the intersection of IPP and the Fox River Trail, the Elgin branch heads toward Wheaton through fields, forest groves, and natural scenery. There is a steep hill in Wayne, about mile 4, with four scenic miles through forest and residential areas to Prince Crossing Rd. There, the IPP crosses the 12-mile DuPage segment of the Great Western Trail. Continue on the Elgin branch for three more pleasant miles, and you'll connect with the Geneva Spur of the IPP (which extends 11 miles west to the suburb of Geneva).

During the last section of this Elgin segment you'll pass through the Lincoln Marsh Natural Area. Then, there's a mile to Volunteer Park in Wheaton.

Parking and Trail Access

Access the Aurora trailhead by taking Interstate 88 to Farnsworth Avenue South; go 1.1 miles. Turn right on Indian Trail, and after 1.5 miles turn left on Aurora Avenue for just a little less than a mile. Take a right onto Illinois Avenue, and the trailhead is on the right just before the Fox River.

To reach the Maywood endpoint from Interstate 290, take 1st Avenue North. The trail is about 0.3 mile north on the left between Quincy and Wilcox Streets; no parking available.

To reach the Wheaton trailhead, take Interstate 355 to Roosevelt Road. Go west 3.6 miles. Turn right on West Street and go 0.4 mile. Make a left onto Liberty Drive. The trailhead is on the right just past a parking garage. Park on the street or in the garage.

The Elgin trailhead is on Raymond Street in Elgin. From Interstate 90 take the State Street exit south for 2.7 miles. Turn left onto National Street and go just under 0.5 mile, and then turn right onto Raymond Street. The trailhead is about 1.3 miles ahead on the right between Purify Drive and Riverview Drive.

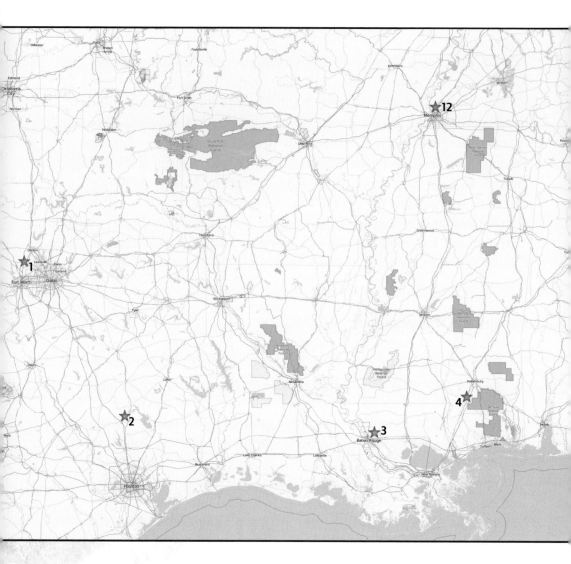

7.3 SOUTH

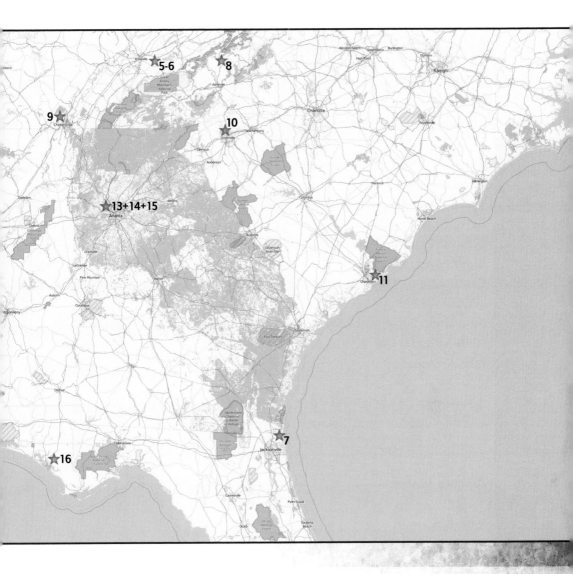

North Shore Trail

Fort Worth/Grapevine, TX

Location Info

Closest City: Fort Worth, TX
Closest Airport: Dallas/Fort Worth International Airport (DFW)
Closest Interstate: 35, 635
Coordinates: Fort Worth, TX–Simmons Rd. Entrance 32.59.51.46N 97.05.20.78W
Best Time: September-May
High Altitude: 600 ft
Low Altitude: 567 ft

Attractions:

* Dallas Arboretum & Botanical Gardens
* Fort Worth Stockyards National Historic District

Parking & Access: -

Websites:
www.nttr.org/html/northshore.htm

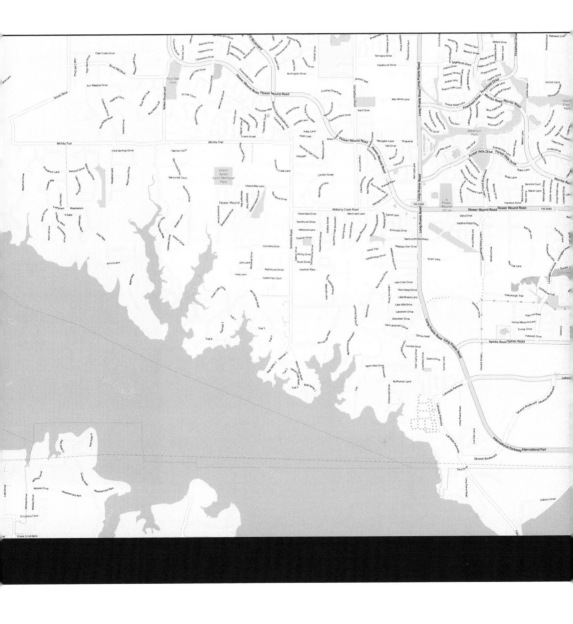

The Terrain

Located only about 20 minutes from DFW airport, Jeff has run on this trail several times when flight schedule would allow. The lake was constructed as a reservoir in 1952 when the Army Corps of Engineers dammed Denton Creek.

The 18-mile Northshore Trail is the most popular multipurpose trail in the Dallas/Fort Worth metroplex—and probably the best trail loop in the area, also. It's popular with trail cyclists, so be aware—especially on the 4-mile out-and-back shared section. The east side is interesting and runnable, whereas the west side is tougher with more debris. If you run on the west side, be sure to run through the bamboo forest, for a special experience.

There are three trailheads: Rockledge Park (Jackson Pavilion), Murrell Park (MADD Shelter), and Twin Coves Park. Each park has water fountains. Bathrooms can be found at Rockledge and Murrell. A parking fee will apply at Rockledge Park.

The trail can be slippery when wet. Like other trails in the Dallas/Fort Worth area, the trail will close if there has been rain. Check the DORBA trail conditions page before heading out there.

Huntsville State Park

Huntsville, TX/Sam Houston National Forest

Location Info

Closest City: Huntsville, TX
Closest Airport: Huntsville International Airport (HSV)
Closest Interstate: 45
Coordinates: Huntsville, TX–Main Entrance 30.37.42.23N 95.31.33.41W
Best Time: September-May
High Altitude: 360 ft
Low Altitude: 350 ft

Attractions:
* Sam Houston Statue
* Texas Prison Museum

Parking & Access: Several parking options available.

Websites:
www.tpwd.state.tx.us/state-parks/huntsville

The Terrain

The 129-mile Lone Star Trail winds through the piney woods of loblolly and short leaf pine trees with some trails along Lake Raven. This area includes the Sam Houston National Forest.

The Rocky Racoon races are held here: 50K, 25K, and 10K in November and a 100-miler in late January, early February.

History: Local citizens voted to construct a recreation area in the 1930s. The CCC (Civil Conservation Corps) was brought in to assist local groups. In 1940, unusually heavy rains caused a failure of the Lake Raven Dam. It was not repaired until after World War II, when the park was developed.

Parking and Trail Access

From the park there are several options. Water and bathrooms are available. An entrance fee will apply.

Hooper Road Park

Baton Rouge, LA

Location Info

Closest City: Baton Rouge, LA
Closest Airport: Baton Rouge Metropolitan Airport (BTR)
Closest Interstate: 110
Coordinates: Baton Rouge, LA 30.31.58.63N 91.07.26.14
Best Time: September-May
High Altitude: 100 ft
Low Altitude: 70 ft

Attractions:

* Old Louisiana State Capitol Building
* USS Kidd
* Louisiana State University Campus

Parking & Access: Parking lot near the trailhead.

Websites:
bramba.org/trails.php

The Terrain

Located near the airport, this 10-mile dirt trail is a delightful network of paths along streams and through forest, with short ups and downs to keep the run interesting. There's also a connection to the Comite River trails, which adds five miles.

After even one rainstorm the trail can be slippery. A heavy downpour and certainly several days of rain can produce flooded portions and muddy quagmires. This is also a mountain bike trail, so be aware.

Directions to trail head:
Take Interstate 110 to the Baton Rouge Airport Exit. Get on Harding Blvd. north toward Plank Road. Harding Blvd. changes name to Hooper Road at the first traffic light. Turn left on Cedar Glen to the dead end, and turn right on Guynell. The entrance is two blocks away. From the parking lot, the trailhead is on the left.

Bethel Mountain Bike Trail

Saucier, MS/Desoto National Forest

Location Info

Closest City: Biloxi, MS
Closest Airport: Gulfport-Biloxi International Airport (GPT)
Closest Interstate: 10
Coordinates: Saucier, MS 30.36.05.12N 88.56.41.44W
Best Time: September-May
High Altitude: 110 ft
Low Altitude: 40 ft

Attractions:

* Biloxi Beach
* Shoreline Casinos
* Beauvoir

Parking & Access: Parking available near the trailhead.

Websites:

trails.mtbr.com/cat/united-states-trails/trails-mississippi/trail/bethel-roadtrails/prd_168737_4558crx.aspx

The Terrain

Containing about 37 miles of trails, this is reported to be the longest trail system in Mississippi. There are actually two loops: 18 miles and 19 miles. It was originally developed in the 1970s as an off-road motor vehicle course (dirt bikes and ATVs), and occasionally you'll see some on the trail—as well as occasional mountain bikes.

This runs through forests, along a beautiful stream, and through natural vegetation. It is composed of dirt with some sandy segments and is generally runnable after most rains—compared with other trails in the area.

There's a bathroom at the trailhead, and a user fee may apply (unmanned).

Parking and Trail Access

From Interstate 10, north of Biloxi, take exit 46 (old Highway 67) for two miles. Turn right on Highway 15 for about nine miles. Be alert for yellow caution arrows on the right. About half a mile after the arrows, turn left on a dirt road. A clue is a USFS bike trail marker. Go about two miles, and you'll find the trailhead on the left.

Elkmont Loop Trail

Great Smoky Mountains National Park, TN (GSMNP)

Location Info

Closest City: Knoxville, TN
Closest Airport: McGhee Tyson Airport (TYS)
Closest Interstate: 40
Coordinates: Great Smoky Mountain National Park, TN–Jakes Creek Trail 35.39.07.75N 83.34.53.24W
Best Time: April-October
High Altitude: 4000 ft
Low Altitude: 2140 ft

Attractions:
* Smoky Mountain National Park attractions
* Gatlinburg Shopping and attractions
* Clingman's Dome Lookout

Parking & Access: Parking available at Elkmont Campground.

Websites:
www.protrails.com/trail/446/great-smoky-mountains-national-parkelkmont-loop-and-husky-branch-falls
www.hikinginthesmokys.com/feature.htm

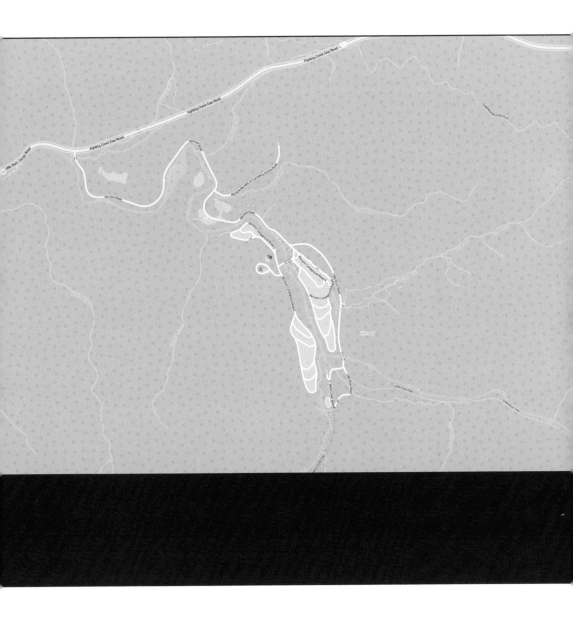

The Terrain

The Elkmont Loop/Husky Branch Falls is a beautiful run through classic Smokey Mountain river environment, about five and a half miles round-trip. A counterclockwise direction is recommended—especially for the downward slant at the end. This is generally a runnable trail, but look for trail debris. The inclines are usually not steep. There are bears in the area, so beware. On the National Park website you'll find information about procedures during bear encounters.

History: The Little River Lumber Company started harvesting lumber in 1901 and built a rail line to from Maryville, TN, to what is now Townsend, TN, to transport the product. In the process, they built the original roads in the area, and many are now trails in the National Park. Colonel Townsend, company owner, sold his acreage to the GSM National Park and ceased operations in 1939. The houses in Elkmont were originally vacation homes but were purchased by the park with a lifetime lease to use the land.

The trail: The Elkmont Campground is the recommended start, at trailheads labeled "Little River" or "Jakes Creek." Going counterclockwise, the Jakes Creek Trail gains elevation gradually in the Elkmont Historic district up to the Cucumber Gap Trail, with a few steep grades (walk breaks), becoming a singletrack. After about three miles, turn left on the Little River Trail (which has a packed dirt surface) to Husky Branch Falls. The trail then heads down gently, along the river and back to the campground.

Cades Cove

Great Smoky Mountain National Park, TN (GSMNP)

Location Info

Closest City: Knoxville, TN
Closest Airport: McGhee Tyson Airport (TYS)
Closest Interstate: 40
Coordinates: Great Smoky Mountain National Park, TN–Loop Entrance 35.36.23.40N 83.46.35.67W
Best Time: April-October
High Altitude: 1946 ft
Low Altitude: 1709 ft

Attractions:

* Smoky Mountain National Park attractions
* Gatlinburg Shopping and attractions
* Clingman's Dome Lookout

Parking & Access: Parking available near park entrance.

Websites:
www.nps.gov/grsm/planyourvisit/cadescove.htm

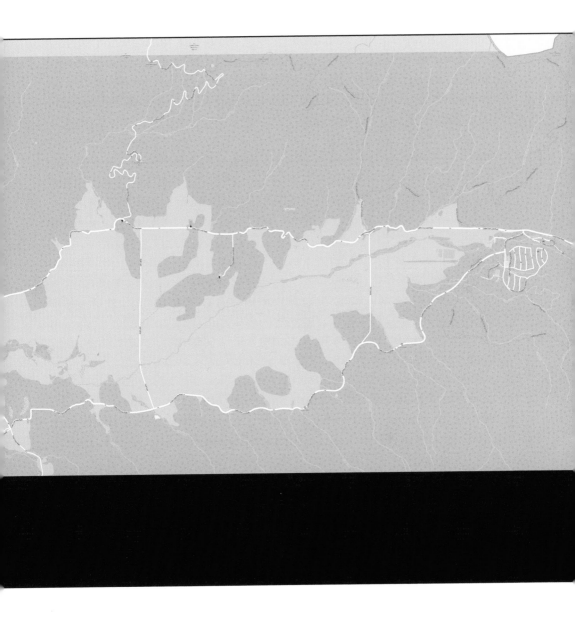

The Terrain

This isolated valley, surrounded by Smokey Mountains, was an early settlement for the pioneers who travelled west in search of their own land. The GSMNP has maintained the homesteads in their natural settings. This beautiful and peaceful 11-mile loop is best run before 10 am, when the road is opened to vehicles. There are several roads that cut through, allowing for a shorter course. Parking is available at the entrance to the cove from Townsend and at the Sugarland Visitor's Center. There is also a five-mile trail (round trip) to Abrams Falls.

History: Cades cove was on one of two main trails used by the Cherokees to go to east and west from what is now North Carolina across the mountains. During the 18th century, the Cherokee had a settlement in the Cove. European traders were using these trails in the mid-18th century, followed by pioneers.

Cades Cove was named after the native, Chief Kade. The settlement was abandoned after the treaty of 1819 when the Cherokees gave up all claim to the Smokey Mountain area. John Oliver and his wife were the first European settlers in the Cove in 1819. Between 1820 and 1835 a number of settlers arrived, setting up farms, a forge, a tub mill, a grist mill, and a moonshine operation—and the community took on a life of its own.

Leading up to and during the Civil War, Blount County, TN, and Cades Cove sided with the abolitionists and then the Union. They suffered a number of attacks by Confederates during the war. It wasn't until the early 1900s that the local economy and population recovered to pre-1860 levels.

Parking and Directions

If headed west on Interstate 40 from North Carolina, take Interstate 40 to Wilton Springs/U.S. 321 south and west exit 440. Turn right and follow U.S. 321 into Gatlinburg. From the first light, it is less than a mile to the park entrance and the Sugarland Visitors Center.

If heading north on Interstate 75 from Georgia or Florida, take exit 81 (S.R.95). Go east on 321 through Maryville and Townsend, where you enter the park from the Townsend entrance, near Cades Cove.

From Knoxville: Take Interstate 40 east and exit 364 S.R. 95. Go east on 321 through Maryville and Townsend, where you enter the park from the Townsend side of the Smokies, near Cades Cove.

Fort Clinch State Park

Fernandina Beach, FL

Location Info

Closest City: Fernandina Beach, FL
Closest Airport: Jacksonville International Airport (JAX)
Closest Interstate: 95
Coordinates: Fort Clinch State Park, FL–Main Parking Lot 30.42.12.50N 81.27.11.47W
Best Time: September-May
High Altitude: 20 ft
Low Altitude: 0 ft

Attractions:

* Atlantic Beach
* Catty Shack Ranch Wildlife Sanctuary

Parking & Access: Parking available at the fort and near Fernandina Beach.

Websites:
www.floridastatepark.org/fortclinch/

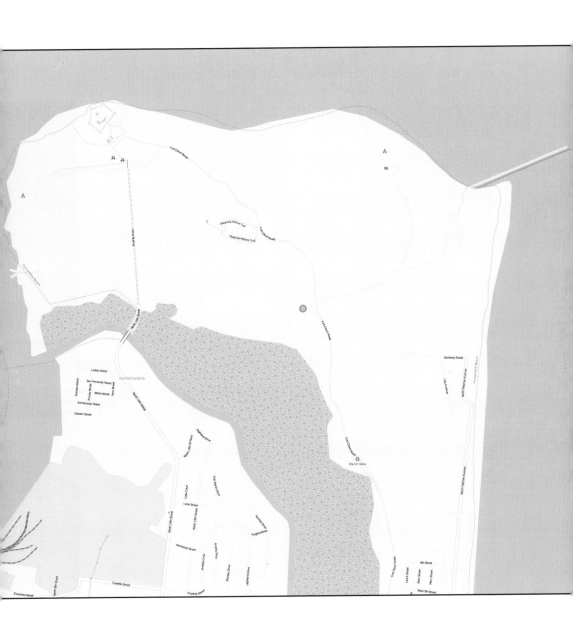

The Terrain

Photos by Becky White

This single-track trail begins at the fort parking lot, running close to the park access road but among trees and natural foliage. At about three miles the trail crosses the road and returns on the other side. You'll pass sand dunes that are among the highest in Florida.

There are also two trail loops at Willow pond, and a usually wide and packed sand beach along the Atlantic and the St. Mary's River. Across the river is Cumberland Island, Georgia. Ancient oaks, sculpted by the wind, twisted cedar trees, and Spanish moss create a unique atmosphere. Often sighted are deer, many birds, including bald eagles, and alligators. We saw one in a creek when these pictures were taken.

History: This was a strategic location to monitor and/or control shipping along the Atlantic coast and the St. Mary's River. In 1736 the Spanish established a military post to protect the northern border of their American real estate: Florida.

In the early 1800s the US erected a fort and named it Fort Clinch in 1847. Confederates took control of the fort early in the Civil War but withdrew in 1862. Union troops took the fort and used it as a base of operations to control the Florida and Georgia coasts. The State Park opened in 1938.

Parking and Trail Access

Parking is available at the fort, and there is a user fee at the park entrance. Free parking is available in nearby Fernandina Beach.

Directions from Interstate 95: Take exit 373 east (also A1A). As you come into the town center of Fernandian Beach, turn right on Atlantic. (This keeps you on A1A and 200.) About half a mile from the beach, you will see Fort Clinch State Park on your left.

Mountains-to-Sea Trail

Asheville, NC/Segment North Carolina Arboretum

Location Info

Closest City: Asheville, NC
Closest Airport: Charlotte Douglas International Airport (CLT)
Closest Interstate: 26, 40
Coordinates: Asheville, NC–NC Arboretum Trailhead 35.30.06.51N 82.35.40.55W
Best Time: April-November
High Altitude: 2510 ft
Low Altitude: 2080 ft

Attractions:
* Biltmore Estate
* Blue Ridge Parkway
* The North Carolina Arboretum

Parking & Access: Various parking opportunities available along the trail (cp. map on website).

Websites:
www.ncmst.org/the-trail/interactive-map/

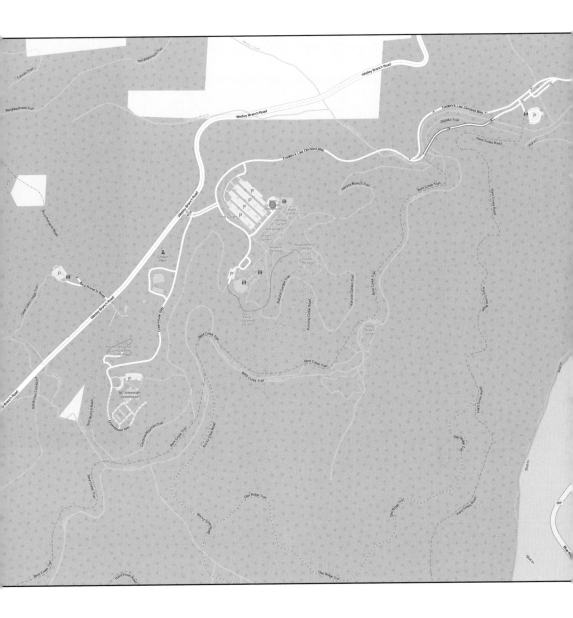

The Terrain

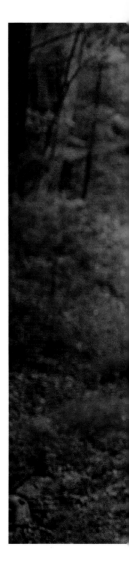

This is an amazing project by the people of North Carolina: A 1,000-mile continuous trail system from the Great Smoky Mountains to the Outer Banks. Each segment of the trail is designed to attract participation from local residents. Supporting this organization is a team of volunteers to construct and maintain the system. A lot of care and pride is involved.

This segment photographed is near the intersection of Brevard Road and the Blue Ridge Parkway, south of Asheville and also near the French Broad River. This URL will allow you to find a segment throughout the length of the 1,000-mile trail.

Monte Sano State Park Trails

Huntsville, AL

Location Info

Closest City: Huntsville, AL
Closest Airport: Huntsville International Airport (HSV)
Closest Interstate: 565
Coordinates: Huntsville, AL–Railroad Bed/Bluff Line Trailheads 34.44.37.73N 86.32.39.96W
Best Time: March-November
High Altitude: 1480 ft
Low Altitude: 1050 ft

Attractions:

* U.S. Space and Rocket Center
* Lowe Mill Arts & Entertainment

Parking & Access: Parking available at the park.

Websites:
www.alapark.com/monte-sano-state-park
www.stateparks.com/monte_sano_state_park_in_alabama.html

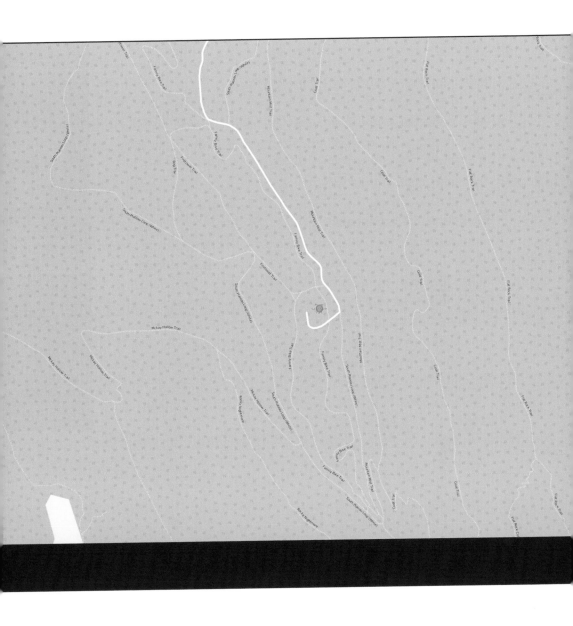

The Terrain

There are over 14 miles of forest trails in this beautiful setting. Park at the visitor center, and you'll find quick access to North Plateau Loop and South Plateau Loop for a gentle warm-up and generally good footing with minimal elevation increase. For those who want to go farther with more of an incline, take the Mountain Mist and McKay Hollow trails.

This protected forest has many interesting plants, including ginseng and wild roses. There are many deer and feral goats. Snakes are occasionally seen but won't harm you unless you challenge them.

Parking and Trail Access

From Interstate 65, take exit to Interstate 565 east (ALT US-72 E, AL-20 E). Continue on Interstate 565 east for approximately 19 miles. Exit onto off-ramp at exit 19C to Washington Street NW. Bear left onto Washington Street NW and travel less than a mile. Turn right onto Pratt Avenue NW and travel less than a mile. Continue onto Pratt Avenue NE and travel a little over a mile. Bear left onto Bankhead Parkway NE and travel approximately three miles. Turn right onto Fearn Street SE and travel less than a mile. Turn left onto Nolen Avenue SE and travel a little over a mile to the park entrance.

Pisgah National Forest

Brevard, NC

Location Info

Closest City: Asheville, NC
Closest Airport: Charlotte Douglas International Airport (CLT)
Closest Interstate: 26, 40
Coordinates: Asheville, NC–US Forest Services Ranger Station 35.17.06.05N 82.43.36.83W
Best Time: April-November
High Altitude: 4500 ft
Low Altitude: 2200 ft

Attractions:

* Biltmore Estate
* Blue Ridge Parkway
* The North Carolina Arboretum

Parking & Access: Pisgah Ranger station.

Websites:
www.hikewnc.info/trailheads/pisgah-national-forest/
www.romanticasheville.com/pisgah_forest.htm

The Terrain

There are so many beautiful trails in the Pisgah National Forest, especially around Brevard! Most have either waterfalls or streams and lots of mountain scenes. Most are runnable, but always be ready to walk through debris on the trail.

Parking and Trail Access
Go to the Pisgah Ranger Station.

Directions:
From Brevard, take US 64 E to US 276. Turn left and follow US 276 N for three miles. Park is located on the right.

Francis Marion National Forest

The Swamp Fox Trail/Charleston, SC

Location Info

Closest City: Charleston, SC
Closest Airport: Charleston International Airport (CHS)
Closest Interstate: 26, 526
Coordinates: Charleston, SC–Awendaw Trailhead 33.02.14.29N 79.37.02.82W
Best Time: September-May
High Altitude: 60 ft
Low Altitude: 10 ft

Attractions:
* Walking tours of the city
* Charleston Waterfront Park
* Boating activities

Parking & Access: Parking available at Awendaw Trailhead (Steed Creek Road).

Websites:
www.sctrails.net/Trails/MAPS/SwampFoxPass%20map.html
www.traillink.com/trail/palmetto-trail—awendaw-passage.aspx

The Terrain

The Swamp Fox Trail is an out-and-back trail which is over 40 miles long. It was developed by Boy Scout leaders and other community organizations in 1968. There are no hills in this tour of marshlands, pine forests, and wetlands—which are very wet after a heavy rain.

History: Outnumbered by British forces, Revolutionary War hero Francis Marion took his ragtag band of patriots into these swampy areas to escape. He was proud of his nickname, "Swamp Fox."

Wildlife: Wild turkey, all types of birds, raccoons, and other furry animals thrive in these swamps. From the southeastern terminus of the Swamp Fox Passage, continue to the coast via the Palmetto Trail-Awendaw Passage. The seven-mile Awendaw Passage marks the end of the Palmetto Trail and runs along the intracoastal waterway, with an overlook at Walnut Grove. Plans are in place to extend this Palmetto Trail to over 400 miles across the state.

Parking and Trail Access

From McClellanville, go south on US 17 about 6.5 miles.

From Awendaw, drive north about three miles and turn at the Buck Hall Recreation Area sign. Then park.

From Charleston, drive north on US 17 to Steed Creek Road (Charleston County S-1032) in Awendaw. Trailhead parking is on the other side of Steed Creek Road.

To the western trailhead: From Charleston, go northeast to Mt. Pleasant. Turn left on SR 41. At Huger, bear left onto SR 402, for three miles and turn right onto Copperhead Road. Go two miles and turn right on Witherbee Road. One half mile later you'll find the parking area and district office.

You can also access the trail from the Awendaw canoe launch at the end of Rosa Green Road or the Swamp Fox trailhead on US 17.

Shelby Farm Trails

Memphis, TN

Location Info

Closest City: Memphis, TN
Closest Airport: Memphis International Airport (MEM)
Closest Interstate: 40, 240
Coordinates: Memphis, TN–Welcome Center Parking 35.08.19.22N 89.49.58.40W
Best Time: March-November
High Altitude: 390 ft
Low Altitude: 280 ft

Attractions:

* Beale Street Entertainment District
* Sun Studio
* National Civil Rights Museum–Lorraine Motel
* Graceland

Parking & Access: Parking available near Visitor Center.

Websites:

www.shelbyfarmspark.org/trails
www.midsouthtrails.com/msta/mapmenu.html

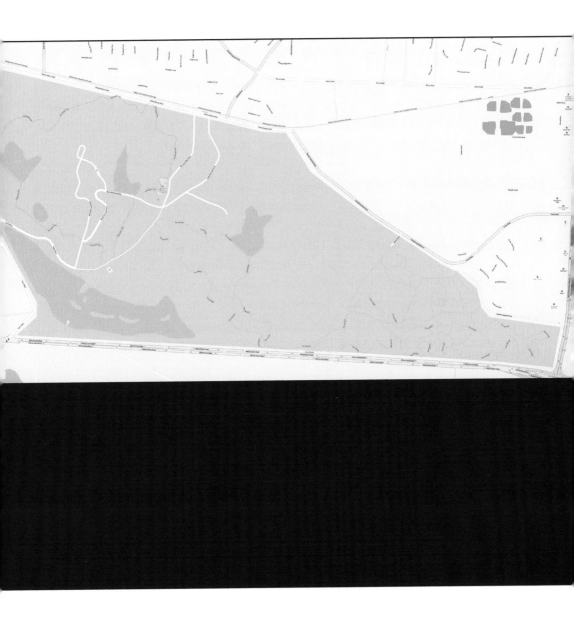

The Terrain

There is great running and walking variety in this popular fitness trail network.

Wolf River Trail meanders for about six miles along this river, weaving between the trees.

The Lucius E. Burch State Natural Area, runs parallel to the Wolf River. These are multipurpose trails, except sections of the Yellow and Blue Trails in the Natural Area, that are designated for walking only.

Cross-country: This five-kilometer loop is used during the fall cross-country season by high school and college teams for workouts and competition.

Shelby Farms Greenline: This six and a half-mile asphalt urban trail connects Shelby Farms Park to Midtown Memphis. The trail currently runs from Tillman Street at Walnut Grove Road in Midtown to Farm Road at Mullins Station Road at Shelby Farms Park. There are access points at Tillman Street, Highland Street, High Point Terrace, Graham Street, Waring Road, Podesta Street, Sycamore View, and Farm Road at Shelby Farms Park.

Chickasaw Trail: This trail is just less than three miles long. It runs across the north section of the park through groves of trees, around three lakes, and through the Woodland Discovery Playground.

South Trail: This is slightly longer than four miles and runs along the south side of Walnut Grove Road. It ends at the Germantown Road trailhead.

Parking and Trail Access

Traveling east on Interstate 40, take the Walnut Grove Road exit east. From Walnut Grove Road, take a left at the Farm Road Intersection. Keep to the right to enter Shelby Farms Park. The Visitor Center will be on your right at 500 North Pine Lake Drive.

Greenline trailheads: Starts at Tillman Street/Walnut Grove Road in Midtown Memphis.

Connections:
Greenline trail links to Shelby Farm Park at Farm Road/Mullins Station.

The Wolf River Greenway connects to the Wolf River Pedestrian Bridge at Shelby Farms Park near the Humphreys/Shady Grove Road intersection. Travel north to head into the park. Continue north to connect to the Shelby Farms Greenline.

Need directions? Call Shelby Farms Park Conservency (901) 767-7275.

Wolf River Trail access: From the Walnut Grove Bridge or the Germantown Road Trailhead.

Kennesaw Mountain Trails

Marietta, GA

Location Info

Closest City: Marietta, GA; Atlanta, GA
Closest Airport: Hartsfield-Jackson Atlanta International Airport (ATL)
Closest Interstate: 75
Coordinates: Kennesaw Battlefield, Atlanta, GA–Main Visitor's Center 33.59.00.03N 84.34.42.29W
Best Time: March-November
High Altitude: 1808 ft
Low Altitude: 980 ft

Attractions:

* Georgia Aquarium
* Martin Luther King, Jr. National Historic Site
* World of Coca-Cola

Parking & Access: Parking areas on Cheatham Hill Road, at the Illinois Monument, and at the visitor center of Kennesaw Battlefield Park.

Websites:
www.nps.gov/kemo/planyourvisit/maps.htm

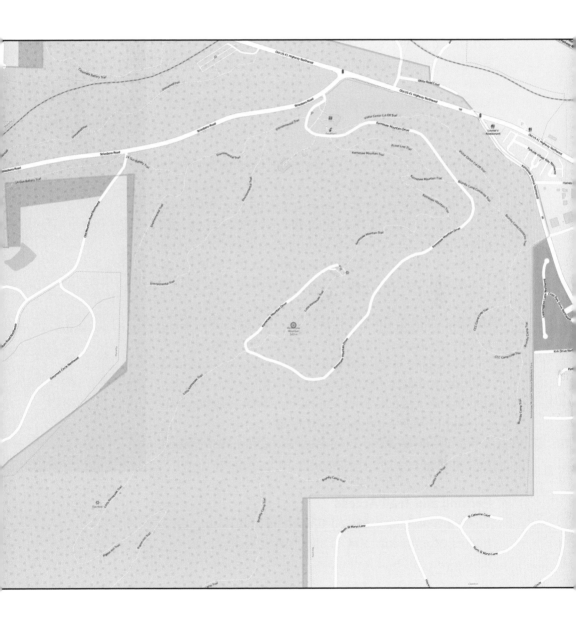

The Terrain

For nine years, Barbara and I lived across the road from the Kennesaw Mountain National Battlefield Park. Our house was in the middle of the battle of Kolb Farm. We enjoyed almost every mile of over 2,000 runs there. Brennan and his brother Westin were introduced to the trails via the first version of the "baby jogger" in which Brennan endured bumps and ruts on treks as long as 11 miles.

This trail network of about 20 miles extends from the Visitor Center at the base of Kennesaw Mountain to Kolb Farm—about seven miles west on the trail, one way. The surface is runnable, but look for rocks and other debris. There are ups and downs, thick forest, and meadows. The environment is similar to the Blue Ridge Mountains, which officially begin about an hour north.

History: During the Civil War, a series of battles were fought on June 27th, 1864. General Sherman led the US forces (100,000), and General Johnston commanded the Confederates (50,000). Instead of out-flanking his opponents, as he had done in previous battles, Sherman decided to attack the heavily dug in Southerners. After losing 3,000 to 1,000 Confederates, Sherman resumed his flanking tactics, taking and burning Atlanta next.

Parking and Trail Access
There are parking areas on Cheatham Hill Road, at the Illinois Monument, and at the Park's visitor center—where you can find trail maps.

Kennesaw Mountain rises 600 feet above the surrounding terrain and offers great views of the area. There are trails to the top as well as a road.

Chattahoochee River National Recreation Area

Sandy Springs/Atlanta, GA

Location Info

Closest City: Sandy Springs, GA; Atlanta, GA
Closest Airport: Hartsfield-Jackson Atlanta International Airport (ATL)
Closest Interstate: 75, 285
Coordinates: Cochran Shoals Trailhead 33.54.12.10N 84.26.40.40W
Best Time: March-November
High Altitude: 1110 ft
Low Altitude: 790 ft

Attractions:

* Georgia Aquarium
* Martin Luther King, Jr. National Historic Site
* World of Coca-Cola

Parking & Access: Parking lot at trailhead available (fee-based).

Websites:
www.nps.gov/chat/index.htm

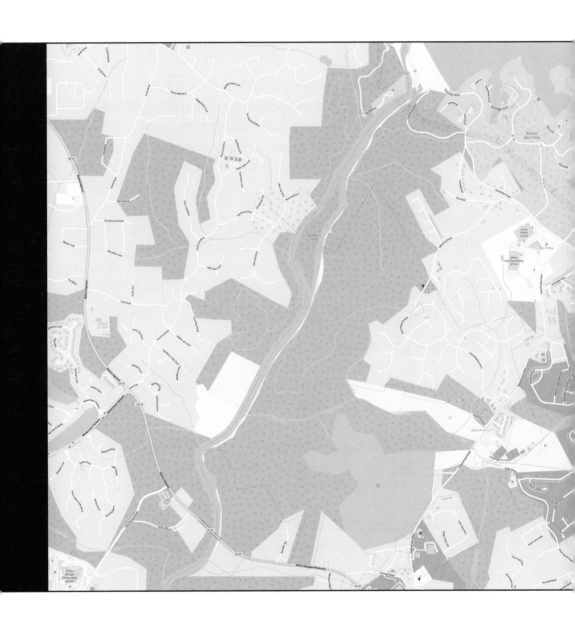

The Terrain

This very popular trail area has a flat and smooth gravel surface three-mile loop along the Chattahoochee River with trails in the adjacent hills. The hills are heavily forested with various species of animals. Surface is generally runnable—but watch for roots and rocky segments.

The flat loop starts immediately from each of the trailheads. Over a mile of the trail is along the river and probably one of the more scenic segments of the Chattahoochee. The elevation rises significantly on the other side and is heavily forested with a few houses visible. Large rocks are visible in the river, giving the appearance of being in the Blue Ridge Mountains, about an hour north of Atlanta.

The hilly loop can be best accessed from the Columns Drive trailhead. Stay on the right side of the loop for about 150 yards and look to the right. A connector trail is visible. This part of the trail system is quite scenic. There is a loop near this access point and an extension out-and-back trail that goes to Sibley Pond and a trailhead off Paper Mill Road.

Parking and Trail Access

North end: From Sandy Springs, go north on Johnsons Ferry Road. Cross the Chattahoochee and turn at the first traffic light, Columns Drive. Trailhead is at the end of the road. Parking fee applies.

South end: From Interstate 75/285 north, go east on Interstate 285 and take the first exit (Exit 22). Go through the first traffic light and turn left at the second light. Cross over Interstate 288 and stay on the same road, crossing Northside Drive. The name changes to Riveredge Lane and is an access road that runs parallel to Interstate 285. Cross over the river and immediately turn right into the parking lot for the trailhead. Parking fee applies.

Piedmont Park

Midtown Area/Atlanta, GA

Location Info

Closest City: Atlanta, GA

Closest Airport: Hartsfield-Jackson Atlanta International Airport (ATL)

Closest Interstate: 75

Coordinates: Ansley Mall (Phidippides Running Center) Trail Parking 33.47.49.92N 84.22.09.78W

Best Time: March-November

High Altitude: 1000 ft

Low Altitude: 870 ft

Attractions:

* Georgia Aquarium
* Martin Luther King, Jr. National Historic Site
* World of Coca-Cola

Parking & Access: SAGE Parking Facility; public transportation to park recommended.

Websites:

www.piedmontpark.org

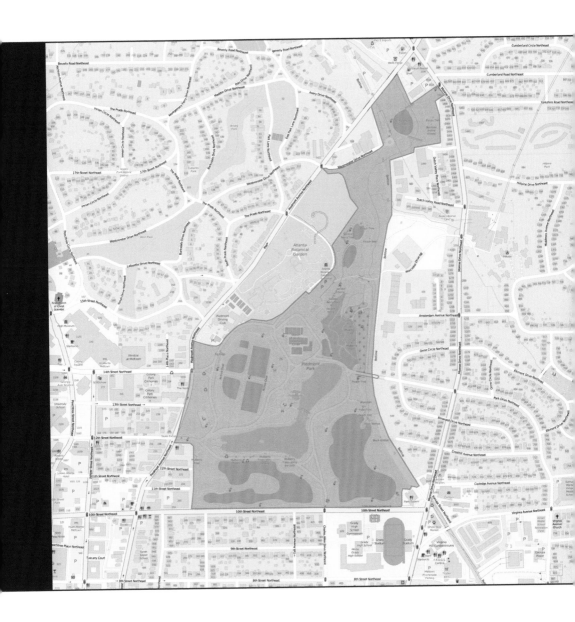

243

This is the crown jewel among Atlanta area parks. The Peachtree Road Race finishes here, as does the Jeff Galloway 13.1. It is located within walking distance of two MARTA stations (Midtown and Arts Center) and located near my running store, Phidippides.

History: Into the late 1800s, this area was still rural, and the land was Dr Benjamin Walker's "gentleman's farm." In 1887 the land was sold to the Gentleman's Driving Club (later the Piedmont Driving Club) for an exclusive club and racing area for those into race horses. The club contracted with the Piedmont Exposition Company to hold fairs and expos. Originally designed by Joseph Forsyth Johnson, it played host to the Piedmont Exposition (1887) and the highly acclaimed Cotton States and International Exposition in 1895. These were "coming out parties" for Atlanta as the leading city of the South.

The park has been a venue for many historic athletic events. Atlanta's first professional baseball team, the Atlanta Crackers, played here from 1902-1904. The oldest rivalry in college football, the University of Georgia vs Auburn, began in Piedmont Park in 1892.

The Trails

There are more than four miles of traffic-free roads to run in Piedmont Park. Atlanta Botanical Garden, which connects to Piedmont Park, has unpaved wooded trails on its north side. There are several paved recreational trails.

The newest extension to Piedmont Park Trails is the Beltline. This is a rail trail which was originally built around 1900 and has been unused for decades. It is currently being rehabilitated as a recreational trail. Free parking is available at Ansley Mall, where my Phidppides store is located. Behind the shopping center is a trail access on an unpaved section of the Beltline that leads directly into Piedmont Park where one can run the trails in the park. To continue on the paved portion of the Beltline, cross Monroe Street at the Park Tavern.

The last two-plus miles of the Jeff Galloway 13.1 are in Piedmont Park, finishing around the beautiful Lake Clara Meer. Our beneficiary is the Piedmont Park Conservancy, which keeps the park in amazing shape.

Point Washington State Park

Blue Mountain Beach, FL

Location Info

Closest City: Santa Rosa Beach, FL

Closest Airport: Pensacola International Airport (PNS)

Closest Interstate: 10

Coordinates: Santa Rosa Beach, FL–Longleaf Greenway Trailhead 30.21.10.56N 86.13.16.06W

Best Time: September-May

High Altitude: 40 ft

Low Altitude: 10 ft

Attractions:

* South Walton Beaches
* Planned Community of Seaside
* Historic Fishing Village of Destin

Parking & Access: Trail system accessible at the parking lot and trailhead on County Road 395.

Websites:

www.freshfromflorida.com/Divisions-Offices/Florida-Forest-Service/Our-Forests/State-Forests/Point-Washington-State-Forest

www.visitsouthwalton.com/activities

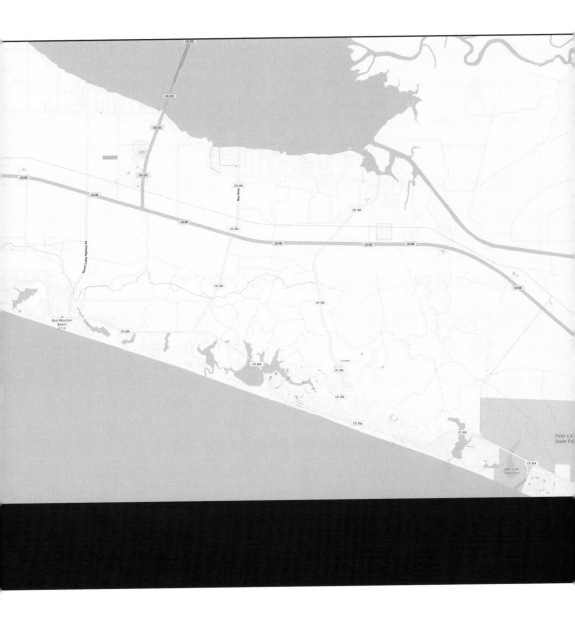

Our Florida running retreats are held here. There's a wonderful balance of natural beauty, laidback atmosphere, good restaurants, and lots of great running venues.

History: While most of the coastal communities in Florida were carved up by developers, this area received help from state officials, such as governor Bob Graham, who wanted to preserve this natural environment so close to the beach.

The Trails

The unpaved roads and trails of Point Washington State Park provide a trail running heaven. There are single-track and double-track options that wind through long leaf pine forests, oaks, cypress, and palmettos. An incredible variety of wildlife has been observed, as well.

The "whitest sand beach in the world" can be loose but usually has a section near the water that is harder packed. There is a recreational trail along the main road (30A), which is about 18 miles long.

The planned community of Seaside is a pleasant and interesting running venue with community parks and natural spaces. The village green is where some of the filming of *The Truman Show* movie took place.

Watercolor, the adjacent St Joe development, has neighborhood parks and unpaved sidewalks that resemble natural paths. There is a wonderful natural dirt trail around Western Lake with great views.

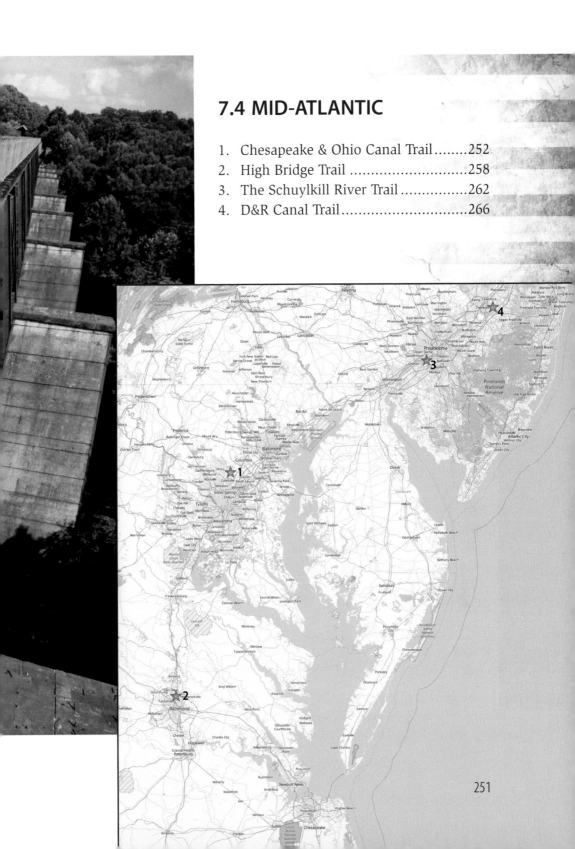

7.4 MID-ATLANTIC

Chesapeake & Ohio Canal Trail

Washington, DC to Cumberland, MD

Location Info

Closest City: Washington, D.C.
Closest Airport: Washington Dulles International Airport (IAD)
Closest Interstate: 81
Coordinates: Williamsport, MD Georgetown Trailhead 38.54.04N 77.03.26.39W, Williamsport Trailhead 39.36.04.34N 77.49.32.29W
Best Time: April-October
High Altitude: 380 ft
Low Altitude: 72 ft

Attractions:
* Smithsonian Museums
* Library of Congress
* Civil War Battlefields (Harper's Ferry, Antietam)

Parking & Access: Fee-based parking at Great Falls National Park entrance. Various access points along the trail.

Websites:
www.nps.gov/choh/index.htm

253

This towpath trail has been designated as a National Historic Park and goes for more than 180 miles along the Potomac River. Its nickname is the C&O Towpath. There are numerous access points in Georgetown, starting at Rock Creek Parkway next to the Watergate. You'll see some of the original locks, spillways and aqueducts, and gatekeeper structures.

History: The C&O Canal was the first major artery for moving freight along the Potomac corridor, and the towpath was heavily used for foot travel in the mid- to late 1800s. It served as an unofficial boundary between northern and southern armies during the American Civil War with on-going skirmishes, raids, sabotage, and movement of troops to and from major battles, including Gettysburg.

After the canal opened, there were bottlenecks in the slackwater sections, so a towpath was constructed and mules provided the power. The southern terminus was originally Great Falls but was extended to Georgetown a year later and then on to the capitol (near the reflecting pool today). Sadly for the investors in the canal, railroads were more efficient and faster.

Along this trail you'll find campgrounds, picnic areas, toilets, vistas, eating establishments, museums and retail shops, historical sites, and B&Bs and motels (including a few restored lock houses). The National Park Service has guidebooks and lots of information about the trail.

Parking and Trail Access

There are numerous access points. The Great Falls National Park entrance has parking, but there is a fee.

High Bridge Trail

Richmond, VA

Location Info

Closest City: Richmond, VA
Closest Airport: Richmond International Airport (RIC)
Closest Interstate: 64, 85
Coordinates: Farmville, VA–River Road Trailhead 37.19.25.25N 78.20.07.16W
Best Time: April-October
High Altitude: 697 ft
Low Altitude: 275 ft

Attractions:

* Jack Daniels Distillery (Lynchburg)
* Monument Avenue (Richmond)
* The White House and Museum of the Confederacy (Richmond)

Parking & Access: Various parking opportunities available along the trail.

Websites:

www.traillink.com/trail/high-bridge-trail.aspx

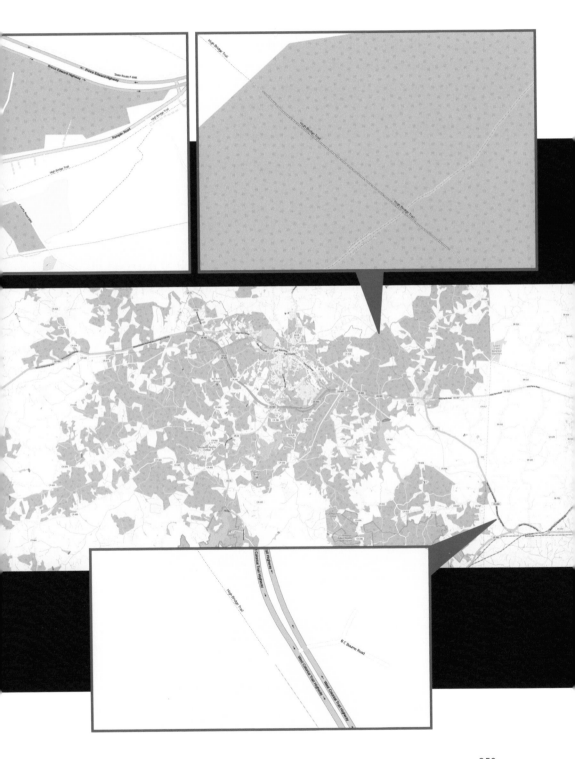

If you like running over bridges, you'll love this half-mile span 125 feet above the Appomattox River. The amazing view is only one of many beautiful experiences on this trail that is about an hour by auto from the capitol of Virginia and the seat of government for the Confederacy during the Civil War, 1861-1865.

History: The bridge was a strategic asset for both sides in this conflict. Both sides tried to destroy and occupy it and did so intermittently. The war ended at nearby Appomattox Court House where General Robert E. Lee surrendered. There are a number of interesting museums and sites in this area.

The Rails to Trails folks recommend a pleasant 4.5 flat trail from the quaint town of Farmville to the bridge on the former South Side Railroad. Noteworthy are the mile marker posts. Those marked "N" state the distance from Norfolk. A "W" reminded the engineer to blow his whistle. There's a parking lot at River Road, about a mile from the bridge.

There are 30 miles of trail extending on either side of the bridge through forests, farms, and the towns of Pamplin City, Prospect, and Rice. The eastern end near Burkeville. Restrooms are available periodically, but drinking water is not. Surface is generally secure, composed of crushed limestone.

Parking and Trail Access
To access the trail, parking is available at the following locations (west to east); a fee is required.
* Near Pamplin: Heights School Road off US Business 460, near trail milepost 168
* In Elam: Off US 460 at Sulpher Spring Road, near trail milepost 164
* In Prospect: Prospect Road off US 460, near trail milepost 161 (wheelchair accessible; designated horse trailer parking)
* In Tuggle: Tuggle Road off US 460 and near US 15 north, near trail milepost 156
* In Farmville: In the municipal lots where the trail intersects Main Street, near trail milepost 150

* In Farmville: Osborn Road, 0.25 mile off N. Main Street, near trail milepost 149 (designated horse trailer parking)
* In Farmville: River Road, 3 miles off N. Main Street, near trail milepost 146
* In Rice: Depot Road, 0.25 mile off US 460, near trail milepost 142 (wheelchair accessible)

The Schuylkill River Trail

Philadelphia, PA to Valley Forge

Location Info

Closest City: Philadelphia, PA

Closest Airport: Philadelphia International Airport (PHL)

Closest Interstate: 76, 78, 276, 476

Coordinates: Philadelphia, PA–Strawberry Mansion Bridge Trailhead 39.59.34.57N 75.11.39.10W, Sullivan Lane Trailhead (Valley Forge) 40.06.34.09N 75.25.21.57W

Best Time: April-October

High Altitude: 140 ft

Low Altitude: 20 ft

Attractions:

* Independence Hall (Philadelphia)
* Eastern State Penitentiary (Philadelphia)
* Valley Forge National Historical Park

Parking & Access: Parking available along the river (see chapter for details).

Websites:

www.schuylkillrivertrail.com/index.php?/trail_head/schuylkill_banks_information_center/

www.visitphilly.com/outdoor-activities/philadelphia/schuylkill-river-trail/#sm.0000sg39aa8otd3ys7d2qc0gajivw

History: In the early days of the US, many historic events took place along or near the path of this trail. The river was the primary venue for transporting people, and cargo business thrived along the banks, where successive industries were established that drove the economy and wealth of the nation. More and more people are commuting to work on the trail—so run/walk single file on the right. Be sure to investigate the Schuylkill Banks Boardwalk that travels over the water, 50 feet from the shoreline.

Valley Forge is where George Washington chose to camp the 12,000 men of the Continental Army through the winter of 1777-1778. Due to the lack of food, clothing, shoes, and medical supplies, about 2,500 soldiers died and another 4,000 were unable to fight. The tough winter, the struggles, and the lack of hope at the time forged the determination of Washington's officers and men whose morale was lifted by spring when France provided some much needed aid. The resulting campaigns turned the tide in the American Revolution.

Downtown segment: Running between the Fairmount Water Works and Locust Street, this 10-mile (one way) linear park is a scenic way to exercise or commute in downtown Philadelphia.

The 27-mile Valley Forge to Philadelphia segment starts at the Philadelphia Museum of Art and runs along the river, through Fairmount Park, and along the Manayunk Canal towpath and a rail trail. Near Valley Forge National Park, there's a link to the 19.5 Perkiomen Trail, with other planned extensions.

Parking and Trail Access

From downtown, go west from city center on Walnut Street, turning left on 23rd Street, right on Spruce Street, and then right on South 25th Street. At Locust Street, to the left you'll find a pathway to the trailhead over the railroad track. Parking is not available here but at other areas along the river area:

* Schuylkill Banks Information Center
* Lloyd Hall

* Girard Avenue Bridge
* Columbia Bridge
* East Park Canoe House
* East Falls
* Manayunk
* Valley Forge

From Interstate 78 (PA Turnpike) to Valley Forge, Exit 326. Take US 422 west to the Audubon/Trooper Exit and turn left off the exit ramp. You'll find parking for the Schuylkill River Trail at the Betzwood Picnic area just ahead.

D&R Canal Trail

Princeton, NJ/New Brunswick, NJ/Trenton, NJ

Location Info

Closest City: Princeton, NJ

Closest Airport: Newark Liberty International Airport (EWR), Philadelphia International Airport (PHL)

Closest Interstate: 95

Coordinates: Princeton, NJ–Washington Rd Trailhead 40.20.20.82N 74.38.47.98W

Best Time: April-October

High Altitude: 60 ft

Low Altitude: 50 ft

Attractions:

* Princeton University
* Princeton Battle Monument

Parking & Access: Various access points and parking available (see chapter).

Websites:

www.traillink.com/trail/delaware-and-raritan-canal-state-park-trail.aspx
njtrails.org/trail/dr-canal-state-park-trenton-to-new-brunswick/

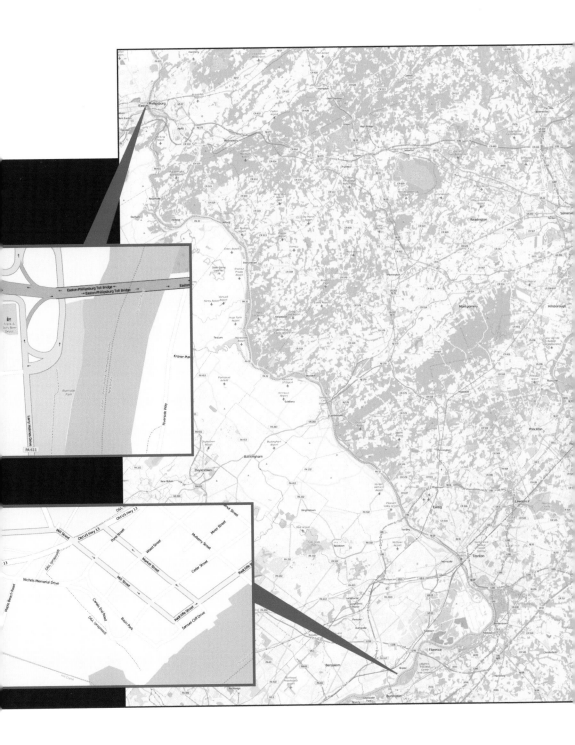

There are three segments to this 77-mile system—the largest in New Jersey—along the Delaware and Raritan Canal. Generally smooth dirt and level, runners and walkers love the scenery and the gentle surface.

History: Built in the 1830s as a transportation corridor between New York and Philadelphia, you'll run along the path used by horses that pulled the barges down the canal. You'll see bridges, locks, and some structures from that era.

Main Canal Towpath, 29 miles in length, is made mostly of dirt and gravel with occasional sections of rough terrain. As in all dirt trails, the surface is slippery and unpredictable in wet weather.

Access points (with parking):
* New Brunswick/Landing Lane Bridge
* Route 287/Somerset
* Bound Brook
* Manville Causeway/Weston
* Amwell Road
* Griggstown Causeway, Princeton
* Alexander Street, Princeton

Feeder Canal Trail is 28.7 miles long, from Trenton near Route 1 to the north end of Frenchtown. Originally designed to bring water from the Delaware River to the Main Canal, the Feeder Canal had a towpath also made of dirt and gravel. Later, a rail line was installed, which explains the firm foundation of this trail.

Access points:
* Washington Crossing State Park
* Lambertville (on-street parking)
* Jimison Farm
* Stockton
* Prallsville Mills
* Bull's Island

D&R Rail Trail heads north from Bull's Island. There are few access points and even shade during the hot time of the year. Built in the mid-1850s by the Belvidere Delaware Railroad, it became part of the Pennsylvania Railroad in the 1870s.

Access points (with parking):
* Bull's Island
* Frenchtown

Note: Periodically, parts of the trail become impassable from floods and other damage. For updates on trail conditions, visit the Canal State Park website *(www.dandrcanal.com/park_index.html).*

The upper portion of the feeder canal follows the Delaware River through many old towns with historical significance. In Trenton, the U-shaped trail has a gap between Mulberry Street and Southard Street. South of Trenton, a disconnected segment runs between John A. Roebling Memorial Park and Hamilton Marshes.

7.5 NEW ENGLAND/ NEW YORK

Central Park

New York City, NY

Location Info

Closest City: New York City, NY
Closest Airport: John F. Kennedy International Airport (JFK)
Closest Interstate: 278
Coordinates: Southeast corner of park 40.45.54.84N 73.58.23.35W
Best Time: April-October
High Altitude: 160 ft
Low Altitude: 70 ft

Attractions:

* Metropolitan Museum of Art
* The National 9/11 Memorial & Museum
* Top of the Rock Observation Deck

Parking & Access: Various garages available near the park.

Websites:
www.centralpark.com/guide/sports/running.html
www.centralparknyc.org

You may have seen the Central Park finish of the New York Marathon or taken a run when on business in NYC. It's the most popular running/ exercise venue in the Big Apple (35 million visitors each year). It's also the most visited urban park in the US. The loop around the outside is about a 10K. But there are a number of other trails in the park—both dirt and paved.

The loop is closed to vehicles for most of the week: Monday through Friday from 10 am to 3 pm and 7 pm to 10 pm and also on the weekends, starting at 7 pm on Friday through 6 am on Monday. (A runner's lane, the innermost recreation lane, is always available—but run against traffic.)

History: Central Park opened in 1857, on 778 acres of city-owned land (it is 843 acres today). The designers were Frederick Law Olmsted and Calvert Vaux, who won a design competition to improve and expand the park with a plan they titled the "Greensward Plan." Construction began the same year, continued during the American Civil War farther south, and was completed in 1873. Central Park is the most visited urban park in the United States.[1]

Running Routes: There are several shortcuts that offer variety. There's a 5-mile loop through the lower and upper sections of the park and a 1.7-mile loop in the southern part of the park by the Tavern on the Green.

The loop around Jaqueline Kennedy Onassis Reservoir is about 1.5 miles with a very slight slope (2%) and spectacular city views. Rule of the road: Stay to the right on this path and run counterclockwise.

There are also two Bridle Path Loops to choose from, both on dirt (Jeff's favorite). The shorter of the two is 1.66 miles and circles around the Reservoir below the cinder path. The Full Bridle Path Loop is 2.5 miles and extends beyond the Reservoir, farther north to the North Meadow fields and across the 102nd Street Transverse. It eventually rejoins the main path after some

---

1   See www.centralpark.com

time on the West Drive. Please note that horses have the right of way on the Bridle Paths, so make sure that you are aware of their location.

Running Groups: The New York Road Runners Club hosts more than 100 running events every year in Central Park and also has a kiosk in the park at the East 90th Street entrance and East Drive by the Engineers' Gate. Open from 6:30 am to 7:00 pm Monday through Friday, 10:00 am to 5:00 pm on Saturday, and 10:00 am to 3:00 pm on Sunday, runners can go here for assistance and information about events.

Access: Central Park is surrounded by four roadways: Central Park North, Central Park South, Central Park West, and Fifth Avenue. There are four plazas on each corner of the park: Frederick Douglass Circle on the northwest, Duke Ellington Circle on the northeast, Columbus Circle on the southwest, and Grand Army Plaza on the southeast. There are also four transverse roadways: 65th–66th Streets, 79th–81st Streets, 86th Street, and 96th Street. The park has three roadways that travel it vertically: West Drive, Center Drive, and East Drive.

The New York City Subway IND Eighth Avenue Line runs along the western edge of the park, with a transfer station to the IRT Broadway – Seventh Avenue Line at Columbus Circle. In addition, the IRT Lenox Avenue Line has a station at Central Park North and 110th Street. From there the line curves southwest and west under the park and heads west under 104th Street, and the BMT Broadway Line has a station at Fifth Avenue and 59th Street.

Walden Pond Trail

915 Walden Street/Concord and Lincoln, MA

Location Info

Closest City: Lincoln, MA
Closest Airport: Boston Logan International Airport (BOS)
Closest Interstate: 95, 495
Coordinates: Walden Pond–Main Parking Lot 42.26.26.74N 71.20.02.46W
Best Time: April-October
High Altitude: 360 ft
Low Altitude: 160 ft

Attractions:

* Freedom Trail
* Boston Tea Party Ships & Museum
* North End Historic District

Parking & Access: Parking available (see chapter for further details).

Websites:
www.mass.gov/eea/agencies/dcr/massparks/region-north/walden-pond-state-reservation.html
www.walden.org

Henry David Thoreau ironically made Walden Pond famous by portraying his stay there (1845-1847) as a restorative, transcendental experience. Many runners will be impressed that Jeff's friend Bill Rodgers (four-time champion of both NYC and Boston Marathons) lives nearby and likes to run there.

The Trails: The loop around the lake is 2.5 miles, but there are extension trails in the State Park. There is a parking fee of $5, and many runners and hikers bring a picnic.

History: Geologically, this is a "kettle hole" created as the great glaciers retreated, 10,000-12,000 years ago. Frederic Tudor, The Ice King, cut ice from Walden Pond and created a business of shipping it to Charleston, New Orleans, the Caribbean, and even India. Thoreau observed the Tudor Ice Company operations one winter: "The sweltering inhabitants of Charleston and New Orleans, of Madras and Bombay and Calcutta, drink at my well ... The pure Walden water is mingled with the sacred water of the Ganges."

Thoreau's mentor, Ralph Waldo Emerson, owned the property and let Thoreau live out his transcendental experience which inspired him to write the iconic book *Walden*. Many credit him with being the first environmentalist. On the trail route you can see the foundation of the cabin and a replica of what it was like (very basic).

From Route 95/128: (north and south, west of Boston area) Take exit 29B onto Route 2 west, at third set of lights, take a left onto Route 126 south. Parking is a quarter of mile down on left.

The Island Line Trail

Burlington, VT

Location Info

Closest City: Burlington, VT
Closest Airport: Burlington International Airport (BTV)
Closest Interstate: 89
Coordinates: Burlington, VT–Downtown Burlington Trailhead 44.28.36.72N 73.13.16.15W
Best Time: May-September
High Altitude: 200 ft
Low Altitude: 100 ft

Attractions:

* Church Street Marketplace
* Burlington Farmer's Market

Parking & Access: Trail parking at Airport Park on Colchester Point Road.

Websites:

www.localmotion.org/island_line_bike_ferry
www.trailfinder.info/trails/trail/island-line-trail

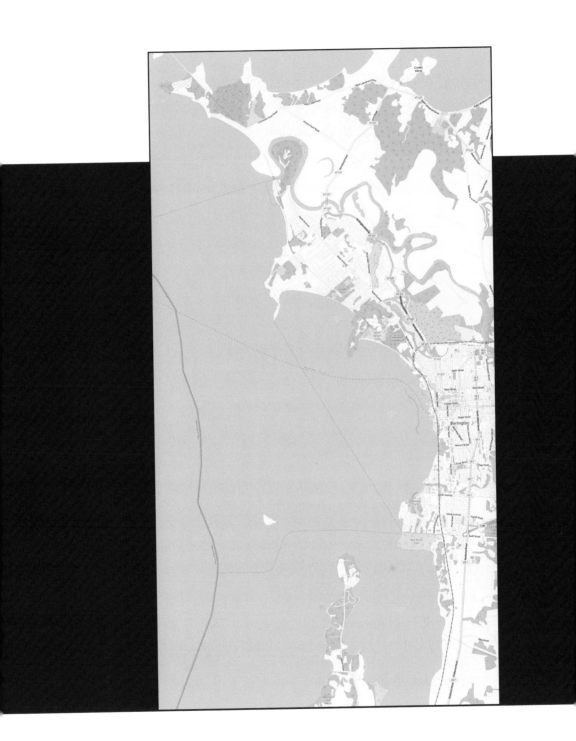

This beautiful rail trail along Lake Champlain is about nine miles in one direction with extensions, if desired. It goes along the lakefront past downtown Burlington then runs through several parks with great views of the lake and the Adirondack Mountains. At the north end, you can run on a causeway composed of marble from the area—right out into the lake.

Official start: Oakledge Park trailhead on Flynn Street in south Burlington. Parking is best at this location, but the trail can be accessed at the following locations (parking fees may apply).

2.1 miles: Union Station trailhead on King Street

3.4 miles: North Beach Park trailhead (seasonal snack bar)

5.1 miles: Leddy Park, Burlington's largest park

Winooski River Bridge: This is a beautiful span—with a half-mile elevated boardwalk across the Delta Park flood plain.

Then there is a brief run through residential neighborhoods and airport park.

Causeway: Built in 1900 atop huge marble boulders, the 2.5-mile raised rail bed slices across Lake Champlain for unparalleled views. As you sail along the crushed stone surface, you'll have a sense of skimming the water's surface. The causeway ends abruptly out on the lake, where a seasonal ferry operated by Local Motion (www.localmotion.org/programs/islandline/bike-ferry) connects with South Hero Island.

Parking and Trail Access

To reach the Oakledge Park trailhead in Burlington, take Interstate 89 to Exit 13 and follow Interstate 189 south to US Route 7. Turn right on US Route 7 north, then left on Flynn Avenue. Follow Flynn to its end and look for signs to Oakledge Park.

To reach the Airport Park trailhead in Colchester, take Interstate 89 to Exit 17 (US Route 2). Follow signs for US Route 2/US 7/Lake Champlain Islands/Colchester. Turn right onto Theodore Roosevelt Highway./Route 2. Continue for three miles before turning right on Bay Road, and then take another right onto West Lakeshore Drive. West Lakeshore becomes Holy Cross Road and then Colchester Point Road. Trail parking is on the right at Airport Park on Colchester Point Road.

The Presidential Range Trail

Gorham, NH

Location Info

Closest City: Gorham, NH
Closest Airport: Manchester-Boston Regional Airport (MHT)
Closest Interstate: 93
Coordinates: Gorham, NH–Gorham Trailhead 44.22.00.11N 71.12.44.86W
Best Time: May-September
High Altitude: 1500 ft
Low Altitude: 890 ft

Attractions:

* Mt Washington
* Santa's Village (Jefferson)

Parking & Access: Parking available in Whitefield, in Randolph at the Castle Trailhead, and at Route 2 in Gorham.

Websites:

trailsnh.com/lists/New-Hampshire-Presidential-Range.php

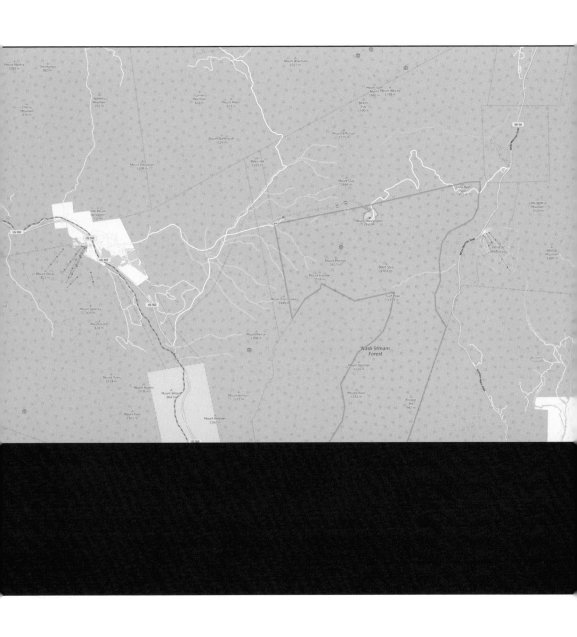

This trail shows off classic New England scenery at its best. Gorham is surrounded by the Presidential Range Trail of the beautiful White Mountains (peaks are named for the early US presidents). Originally constructed by the St. Lawrence and Atlantic Railroad (later called the Grand Trunk Railway), the 18-mile section through Gorham and nearby towns shows off the Androscoggin River, going by quaint shops and historic buildings, providing great vistas of the mountains.

History: Original settlement in the area was in the 1770s with the founding of Gorham in 1802. The railroad was built in the 1850s and expanded local business in logging and various mills. Tourism took off with the opening of the carriage road to the top of Mount Washington in 1861 and is still a major industry today. There is a popular road race to the summit on this road every year.

This dirt and gravel trail runs between Gorham and Cherry Pond, a great area for bird watching. It runs the borders of the White Mountain National Forest and goes through the Silvio O. Conte National Fish and Wildlife Refuge. Generally a smooth surface, the best surface is between Gorham and Jefferson Notch Road Bridges near Cherry Pond take you through the marshland to the White Mountain Regional Airport.

Parking and Trail Access

Parking is available at Hazen Road in Whitefield, at Route 2 in Randolph at the Castle Trailhead, and at Route 2 in Gorham just past Jimtown Road.

Air Line State Park Trail

Northeast, CT

Location Info

Closest City: Colchester, CT; Hartford, CT
Closest Airport: Bradley International Airport (BDL)
Closest Interstate: 910, 395
Coordinates: Colchester, CT–CT 149 Park and Ride 41.35.24.80N 73.24.41.55W
Best Time: May-October
High Altitude: 600 ft
Low Altitude: 180 ft

Attractions:

* Mohegan Sun & Foxwoods Casinos
* Mark Twain House & Museum
* Gillette Castle State Park

Parking & Access: Various parking opportunities available (see chapter).

Websites:

www.traillink.com/trail/air-line-state-park-trail.aspx
www.ct.gov/deep/cwp/view.asp?a = 2716&q = 479336&deepNav_GID = 1650

This delightful 53-mile rail trail offers a secure and generally smooth surface as you run through the forests of Connecticut. There are two gaps: in Putnam and in Willimantic. At the Connecticut and Massachusetts border, there's a connection to the Southern New England Trunk Line Trail which goes for another 22 miles.

History: Built in the 1870s, this was the premier way to travel between New York and Boston, following the shortest and fastest route. The best engineering went into constructing this rail line, and the best engines and cars were used—including the finest Pullman Palace Car luxuriously fashioned in white and gold.

Of interest:

* A 3.4-mile spur, slightly rougher, leads into Colchester, through a hemlock forest.
* Within the first mile at the East Hampton (south) side of the trail you'll find two seasonal waterfalls.
* Two long viaducts (over 1,000 feet each) can be found a little farther north, and one is more than 150 feet above the valley.
* Traillink.com notes: "The trail is part of a massive trail network known as the East Coast Greenway, which will connect communities along the Eastern seaboard from Maine to Florida."

Parking and Access

North end: Parking is available at the Goodwin State Forest Conservation Center on Potter Road off Route 6 in Hampton.

East Hampton end: On the south end of the trail, take State Route 2 to Exit 13 and follow State Route 66 south for four miles. Turn left for half a mile on State Route 196/Lakeview Street, turning left on Flanders Road. Drive 25 mile, turning right on Smith Street, and the trailhead is on the left.

Another trailhead is available at the junction of State Routes 207 and 85 in Colchester. Take Route 2 to Exit 18, follow State Route 16 half a mile south 0.5 mile, then turn left on Route 85. The parking lot is four miles down on the left.

A quirky restaurant to visit is: "Harry's Place" in Colchester—the original burger shack.

Acadia National Park

Bar Harbor, ME

Location Info

Closest City: Bar Harbor, ME
Closest Airport: Boston Logan International Airport (BOS)
Closest Interstate: 95
Coordinates: Bar Harbor, ME–Eagle Lake trailhead 44.22.39.22N 68.15.06.70W
Best Time: May-October
High Altitude: 600 ft
Low Altitude: 100 ft

Attractions:

* Land Bridge to Bar Island trail
* Cadillac Mountain Summit
* Bar Harbor Village

Parking & Access: Pass for private vehicles required to enter the park (fee-based).

Websites:

www.acadianationalpark.com/trails/
www.nps.gov/acad/index.htm

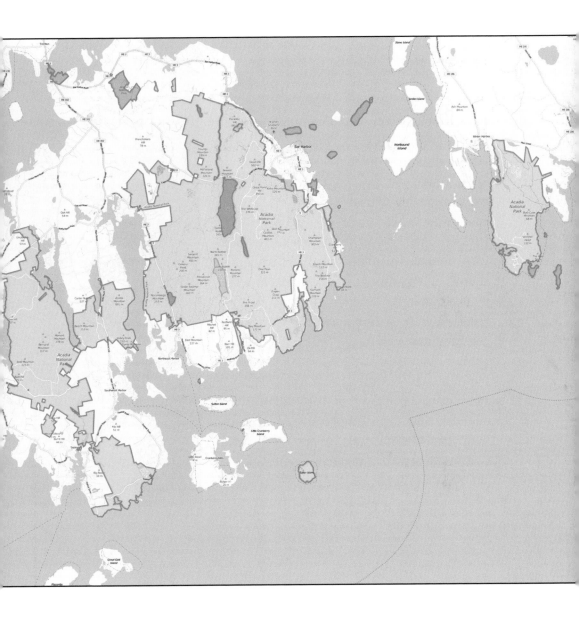

There are more than 100 miles of trails in this 47,000-acre park overlooking the Atlantic Ocean. Over 50 miles of smooth carriage trails were carved out of the beautiful but rugged Maine coastal landscape by philanthropist John D. Rockefeller, Jr. under the design of landscape architect Beatrix Farrand.

Be prepared for a series of vistas and panoramas of incredible beauty. While the trails are well marked, the network is so expansive that you will need a map from the visitor center to know where you are. The park is home to a wide variety of wildlife.

History: Originally called Lafayette National Park, after the famous Frenchman who gave support to the Amerian Revolution, in 1929, it was renamed Acadia after the historic French colony in this area. The Rockefeller contributions were made between 1915 and 1933.

The quaint local town of Bar Harbor offers authentic New England and Maine atmosphere, with unique restaurants, shops, and B&Bs. Camping is available in the National Park.

Rockefeller State Park

Tarrytown, NY (30 miles north of New York City)

Location Info

Closest City: Tarrytown, NY; New York City, NY
Closest Airport: John F. Kennedy International Airport (JFK)
Closest Interstate: 287
Coordinates: Tarrytown, NY–Visitors center 41.06.42.58N 73.50.12.00W
Best Time: April-October
High Altitude: 500 ft
Low Altitude: 150 ft

Attractions:

* Kykuit
* Sleepy Hollow Cemetery

Parking & Access: Vehicle entry fee charged.

Websites:

cnyhiking.com/NYSP-Rockefeller.htm
nysparks.com/parks/59/details.aspx

During the late 1800s, William Rockefeller and John D. Rockefeller bought over 1,000 acres, including the Aspinwall estate—200 acres and a castle, Rockwood—from the heirs of William Henry Aspinwall. Before the year 2000, the Rockefeller family had donated over 1,400 acres of land to the state for this park. There are more than 40 miles of trails through fields, forest, and wetlands and along lakes and over wood and stone bridges.

In 1893, John D. Rockefeller bought land at Pocantico Hills. By 1999 over 1,400 acres of land was donated to the state from the heirs of the Rockefellers.

Visitors can now explore this scenic property in Westchester County known as Rockefeller State Park Preserve. Approximately 30 miles north of the hustle and bustle of New York City, the Preserve is a great spot for strolling, jogging, hiking, horseback riding, cross-country skiing, and snowshoeing.

The Old Croton Aqueduct Trail passes along the eastern end of the park. The Old Croton Aqueduct Trail significantly extends trail access to Sleepy Hollow and Tarrytown, where there is a Metro North train station.

This outdoor paradise exists due to the generosity of the Rockefeller family. The awesome feature of the Preserve is the system of carriage roads built by John D. Rockefeller Jr. Designed to complement the landscape, the carriage roads, many of which are handicap accessible, allow visitors to explore over 40 miles of trails and enjoy the natural wonders of the area. These scenic paths wind through wetlands, woodlands, meadows, and fields and past streams, rivers, and lakes while traversing wood and stone bridges.

One road passes by the foundation of Rockwood Hall, once the 220 room home of William Rockefeller. A panoramic view of the Hudson River remains a spot of beauty for all who visit. Trail maps (with distance and grade descriptions) of all the carriage roads and equestrian permits are available at the Preserve Office.

Credits

Cover design, layout and typesetting:	Andreas Reuel, Aachen
Inside pages:	©Thinkstock/iStock/Piotr Krześlak –US Flag– on pages 11, 25, 29, 37, 41, 49, 63, 159, 185, 251, 271
Photographs:	All photographs by Brennan Galloway except the following:

Reg Regalado (p. 51)

Kevin Hall & Rebecca Coolidge (p. 53)

Tom Robertson (p. 55)

Mike McBride/GOAL Foundation (p. 57)

Mark Coffey/Action Sports Images (p. 59)

Straley Photopraphy, Barry Rabinowitz & Michael Kelly (p. 60-61)

Alex O'Nelio (p. 175)

Don Williams with Don Shutters (p. 179)

Becky White (p. 212)

Copyediting:	Elizabeth Evans, Kristina Oltrogge

MORE BOOKS BY JEFF GALLOWAY

Jeff Galloway

RUNNING – GETTING STARTED

Galloway offers an easy, step-by-step program. Tips are included on nutrition, staying motivated, building endurance, shoes, stretching, strengthening, and much more. Learn how to run while reducing and eliminating the aches and pains suffered during most training programs.

5th revised edition

240 p., in color,

51 photos, 4 illus.

paperback, 6 1/2" x 9 1/4"

ISBN: 9781782550549

$ 16.95 US/$ 29.95 AUS

£ 12.95 UK/€ 16.95

All information subject to change © Thinkstockphotos/iStock_Ivanko_Brnjakovic

MEYER & MEYER Sport
Von-Coels-Str. 390
52080 Aachen
Germany

Phone   +49 02 41 - 9 58 10 - 13
Fax   +49 02 41 - 9 58 10 - 10
E-Mail   sales@m-m-sports.com
Website   www.m-m-sports.com

All books available as E-books.

MEYER
& MEYER
SPORT